Guide to the Mesoamerican Gallery at the University of Pennsylvania Museum of Archaeology and Anthropology

Frontispiece. View of the Mesoamerican Gallery with Piedras Negras Stela 14 (left) and Caracol Stela 5 in the background and Caracol Stela 6 in the foreground.

Guide to the Mesoamerican Gallery at the University of Pennsylvania Museum of Archaeology and Anthropology

Elin Danien

University of Pennsylvania Museum of Archaeology and Anthropology

CIP data on file at the U.S. Library of Congress

ISBN: 1-931707-28-6 cloth
ISBN: 1-931707-29-4 pbk

Printed in the United States of America on acid-free paper

To the memory of J. Alden Mason and Linton Satterthwaite, the curators who installed the Museum's first Mesoamerican Gallery.

Contents

Illustrations

Foreword

The Mesoamerican Gallery has been located in the Lower Fitler Pavilion of the University of Pennsylvania Museum of Archaeology and Anthropology since the 1930s. When the University of Pennsylvania Museum opened in 1899, collections from Borneo were displayed in this gallery. In the 1920s these were replaced by cases exhibiting African and Oceanian artifacts.

By 1930 the gallery held casts of carved reliefs from the Temple of Jaguars at Chichen Itzá, Mexico, hand painted by Adela Breton. Soon thereafter, the Museum began research at Piedras Negras, Guatemala, one of the first large-scale excavation projects in the Maya lowlands. As part of its agreement with the Guatemalan government, the Museum removed a number of carved monuments from the site so they could be protected from both the elements and vandalism. In 1933, several of these Piedras Negras monuments were installed in the Lower Fitler Pavilion (the remainder are installed in the Museo Nacional in Guatemala City), and since that time this gallery has been home to the Museum's Mesoamerican collections.

Between 1930 and 1966 the Mesoamerican Gallery underwent three major renovations, each reflecting the Museum's latest research in the Maya area, as well as advances in Mesoamerican archaeology. In 1949 the two American Section curators who had led the Museum's Piedras Negras Project, J. Alden Mason and Linton Satterthwaite, installed the first thematic exhibit, centered on the results of the Piedras Negras research. In 1954 Linton Satterthwaite, Curator of the American Section, oversaw a renovation of the Mesoamerican Gallery to include the display of monuments from the Maya site of Caracol, Belize (then British Honduras).

In 1966 new lighting was installed, displays of artifacts in the wall cases were changed, and the original backdrop of the Piedras Negras Acropolis was replaced by black and white photographic murals of Tikal, Guatemala, reflecting the Museum's ongoing research at that site. The Tikal Project had begun in 1956 under the direction of Edwin Shook, and by the time it ended in 1970 it had revolutionized our understanding of Classic Maya civilization.

In the years since 1966 there were a series of minor changes in the gallery, including extensive new labels for the Maya monuments to reflect advances in the decipherment of Maya writing. The Museum has returned several of the Piedras Negras monuments to Guatemala; those that remain in the gallery are governed by an exchange loan agreement with the Guatemalan government. In fact, by the mid 20th century government regulations in most countries had set new rules for archaeological research, so all excavated artifacts had to remain in their country of origin. Thus the Mesoamerican Gallery—newly renovated in 2000 thanks to a generous donation from Mrs. Elena Kyle and thanks to the skills and efforts of Elin Danien, Research Associate in the American Section and author of this guide—does not include materials from the Museum's precedent-setting research at Tikal or in the Salamá Valley and at Quiriguá (both in Guatemala), and its most recent long-term research in the royal Acropolis of Copán, Honduras.

The results of this research are being published by the Museum, however, so that scholars and people throughout the world can share in the knowledge generated by these projects. That knowledge is also shared with every visitor to the gallery through the exhibits and information they impart about the ancient civilizations of Mesoamerica.

ROBERT J. SHARER
Curator in Charge, American
   Section
University of Pennsylvania Museum
   of Archaeology and Anthropology

Ceremonial basalt metate *and* mano. *Maya (?), Guatemala, Sta Lucia Cotzumalhuapa, Pacific Slope. A.D. 300–800. NA11872/11873. Metate: H. of head 34 cm; L. 19.5 cm; W. 53.5 cm. Mano: L. 86 cm; Dia. at center 10.5 cm. This large ceremonial grinding stone, with its beautifully carved crocodilian head, was collected on the Pacific Coast of Guatemala. It is probably an import, since its style is that of the Chorotegan culture of Costa Rica's Pacific coastal region.*

Acknowledgments

Among the people who provided invaluable help for the gallery renovation on which this book is based, as well as for the book itself, I thank Jeremy A. Sabloff, Williams Director of the University of Pennsylvania Museum of Archaeology and Anthropology, and Robert J. Sharer, Curator in Charge, American Section, who gave the project initial approval and continued support, and Chris Jones, Senior Research Scientist, American Section, whose depth of knowledge provided guidance in innumerable ways.

John Harris, Research Associate, American Section, not only provided detailed translations and descriptions for all the monuments, but helped to drastically edit his own copy when it was apparent that major surgery was necessary, yet never lost his good humor. I urge those interested to read the expanded translations in the monument labels in the gallery.

John Montgomery generously allowed the use of his drawings of the Piedras Negras monuments. The drawings of the Caracol monuments are by Carl Beetz from *The Monuments and Inscriptions of Caracol, Belize* by Carl P. Beetz and Linton Satterthwaite (Philadelphia: University of Pennsylvania Museum, 1981).

Lucy Fowler Williams, Keeper, and William Wierzbowski, Assistant Keeper, American Section, were enthusiastic allies in the development and execution of the gallery renovation. Gillian Wakely, Associate Director for Education, Michele Saland, Coordinator of Volunteer Guides, and all the Mesoamerican Gallery docents offered insight and direction. Senior Registrar Xiuqin Zhou and her staff always accommodated my sometimes difficult research needs. The Exhibits Department—Jack Murray, Designer, Kevin Lamp, Graphics, and Howard Clemenko, Mounts—brought life to my words and reality to my vague concepts with their creativity and visual style. Alessandro Pezzati, Archivist, and Charles Kline, Photo Archivist, provided documents, photographs, and much-needed advice. Virginia Greene, Senior Conservator, and Lynn Grant, Conservator, conserved the objects and assured their proper installation.

This publication was first suggested by Walda Metcalf, Director of Publications, who managed to keep me to a schedule and forced me to adhere to a word limit (no mean feat). Jennifer Quick had the difficult task of designing this guide within a very narrow time frame. The beautiful photographs are the work of Francine Sarin, Head Photographer, and her assistant, Jennifer Chiappardi.

None of this would have been possible without Elena Kyle, whose financial support helped underwrite the gallery renovation, whose prodding kept it going, and whose cry for "Color!" we have tried to follow. As a Museum docent, and as a friend, she is a treasure!

Guide to the
Mesoamerican Gallery at the
University of Pennsylvania Museum
of Archaeology and Anthropology

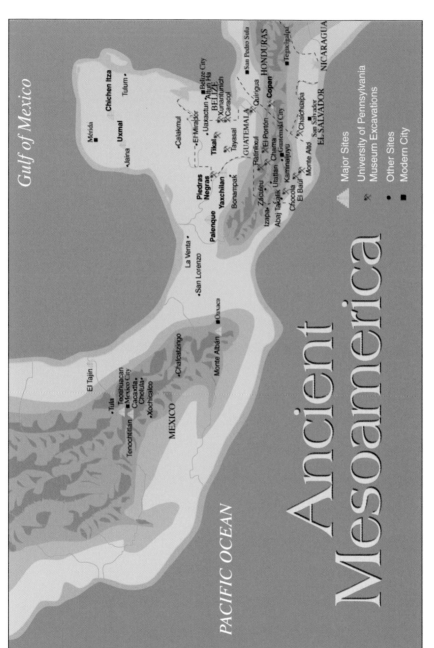

Figure 1. Mesoamerica, with sites of University of Pennsylvania Museum field work mentioned in text indicated by pickax and shovel.

The University of Pennsylvania Museum of Archaeology and Anthropology in Mesoamerica

The Mesoamerican Gallery reflects the long history of research by the University of Pennsylvania Museum of Archaeology and Anthropology into ancient Mesoamerica, the archaeological term given to the area encompassing Central and Southern Mexico, all of Guatemala, Belize, El Salvador, and parts of Honduras, Nicaragua, and Costa Rica (Figure 1). The Museum's research into the early cultures of the region dates to 1912, when Museum Director George Byron Gordon hired Robert Burkitt to excavate on the Pacific Slope and in the highlands of Guatemala. Burkitt's decades-long association with the Museum resulted in a superb collection of well-documented material from that little-known region of Maya civilization.

The Museum's first institutional Mesoamerican excavation was at the rainforest site of Piedras Negras, Guatemala. Museum curators J. Alden Mason and Linton Satterthwaite, the expedition's field directors, had few precedents to guide them in what was a pioneering venture that began in 1931 and continued through eight field seasons. In 1951 and 1953 Satterthwaite called on much that he had learned at

Piedras Negras when he directed the Museum's expedition to Caracol, in Belize, to recover, preserve, and record its sculptured monuments, and to map the site.

The Museum's best-known contribution to Mesoamerican archaeology was its fifteen-year undertaking at Tikal, in the Petén region of Guatemala, from 1956 to 1970. This interdisciplinary excavation, now carried forward by the Guatemalan Institute of Anthropology and History (IDAEH), was conducted on a scale unprecedented for Maya archaeology and became a model for the comprehensive examinations of Maya sites that followed. The Museum's continued commitment to excavation at such notable sites as Chalchuapa, El Salvador, and Copán, Honduras, and to large-scale regional projects in the Salamá Valley and Quiriguá, Guatemala, and Xunantunich, Belize, has added valuable insights to the growing body of knowledge about Precolumbian Mesoamerica.

When the Museum was founded at the end of the 19th century the acquisition of objects was the primary goal for it and other similar institutions. Over time, the practice of archaeology has shifted from the collection of objects for display to a more comprehensive view of the cultures that created those objects, and from a focus on the material culture of the rulers to an attempt to understand the lifeways of all those who had participated in those early cultures. The Museum's collecting practice has changed in similar fashion. Thus, while some of the objects in the gallery were acquired through purchase or gift, many more are the result of early work by Museum archaeologists and anthropologists. Such scientifically based acquisitions bring with them contextual information that allows for more accurate interpretations of cultures long past.

Unfortunately, as knowledge of the beauty of ancient material culture came to be widely recognized, illegal looting became an international problem of major proportions. The University of Pennsylvania Museum was the first institution to take a public stand on what was, and continues to be, a highly controversial subject. On April 1, 1970, the Museum issued what came to be known as the Pennsylvania Declaration, stating that no object would be purchased unless accompanied by a pedigree, including "information about the different owners, place of origin, legality of export, etc." Later that year, the United Nations issued the UNESCO Convention on the Means of Prohibiting the Illicit Import, Export and Transfer of Ownership of Cultural Property. Since then, supporting resolutions have been passed by the Archaeological Institute of America, the Society for American Archaeology, and the American Anthropological Association.

In 1978, the Museum adopted a more stringent acquisitions policy, stating that all undocumented objects made available by gift, bequest, or exchange would be refused if acquired by the owner after 1970, and that the Museum reserved the right to refuse to loan objects to museums or departments suspected of having knowingly violated the UNESCO Convention.

The modern discipline of archaeology has existed for little more than one hundred years, and the scientific investigation of ancient Mesoamerica for less than that. As ethical and national views of archaeology and its rights and responsibilities shift, the role of American archaeologists continues to change. Our archaeologists continue to make exciting discoveries about the civilizations of the past, not only in the Americas but around the world. In the 21st century, however, archaeologists bring back from the field only the knowledge they have gained; the objects, with rare exception, remain in their country of origin.

As archaeologists study material objects to interpret and understand the cultures of those who made and used those objects, so the goal of the Mesoamerican Gallery is to help the visitor glimpse aspects of a culture that began more than three thousand years ago. For those interested in learning more about this fascinating period of human history, a brief reference list is provided at the end of this essay. The gallery display is of material collected during the early years of the Museum's history, but with interpretation based on current theory, fieldwork, and analysis. It is our hope that this guide will help reveal not only the unique characteristics of a civilization long past, but also some qualities of the ancient peoples of Mesoamerica that are universal and relevant to today's world.

MAYA WRITING

This brief outline of Maya writing, arithmetic, and the calendar will be of value in the discussion of the monuments which follows. Much of this is drawn from the 5th edition of *The Ancient Maya* by Robert J. Sharer, and *Understanding Maya Inscriptions: A Hieroglyphic Handbook* (2nd revised edition) by John F. Harris and Stephen K. Stearns.

The hieroglyphic inscriptions on the monuments use a mixed pictographic (a picture representing an object or idea, not anchored to a specific language), logographic (language-specific words or meanings), and syllabic (sounds) writing system. Each glyph consists of a central element, called a main sign, and one or more elements, called affixes, placed around the main sign. In general, the reading order is: prefix, superfix, main sign, subfix, and postfix (Figure 2).

The monument inscriptions are usually read in double columns, from left to right and top to bottom.

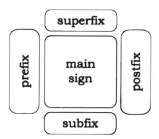

Figure 2. The component parts of a Maya hieroglyph. Glyphs may carry some or all of the affixes (prefix, superfix, subfix, postfix). From Harris and Stearns 1997.

Maya Arithmetic

Our numbering system, known as base-10, uses units of ten. By adding a zero to the right of a digit, we increase that number value by a multiple of ten. The Maya used a base-20 system, increasing number values in multiples of twenty. Numbers were positioned in rows, with the smallest number in the bottom row. By moving the number to an upper row, the Maya increased the value of that number by a multiple of twenty. This system of positional number values required the mathematical concept of zero, perhaps the earliest known use of this concept in the world.

Numbers were written using only three symbols: a shell indicating the completion of a numerical sequence, a dot for one, and a bar for the number five. Numbers up to nineteen were written with a combination of bars and dots (Figure 3). Numbers above nineteen are indicated by a shift in the number position, as discussed above. A dot on the lowest row has a value of one; on the next row up it has a value of twenty; one row further up is 400 (20 x 20), and so on. When recording calendrical data, the Maya sometimes replaced the bar and dot symbols with a series of distinctive deity-head glyphs.

The Calendar

Three of the significant calendrical systems are the 260-day Sacred Almanac, the 365-day Vague Year, both of which cycle endlessly with no beginning and no end (see box), and the Long Count, which starts in the dim past and goes forward in cycles of approximately 5,128 years.

The Sacred Almanac and the Vague Year were used concurrent-

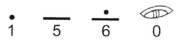

Figure 3. Maya dot (1) and bar (5) numerals. The symbol on the right is the shell.

DETAILS OF THE CALENDAR SYSTEM

The Sacred Almanac

The oldest and most widespread calendrical system in Mesoamerica, called the Sacred Almanac, is composed of 20 named days and 13 numbers (20 x 13 = 260). Each day carries a number from 1 to 13; the number 1 is attached to the first day name, then 2 to the second, and on to thirteen, when the sequence is repeated. Because there are 20 named days and only 13 numbers, days with the same names will carry different numbers as the cycle progresses, as you can see below. This calendar is still used for divinatory purposes in the highlands of Guatemala.

The Maya day names are:

1 Imix	6 Kimi	11 Chuwen	3 Kib	8 Imix
2 Ik	7 Manik'	12 Eb	4 Kaban	9 Ik
3 Ak'bal	8 Lamat	13 Ben	5 Etz'nab	10 Ak'bal
4 K'an	9 Muluk	1 Ix	6 Kawak	11 K'an
5 Chikchan	10 Ok	2 Men	7 Ahaw	12 Chikchan

and so on.

The Vague Year

Another calendrical system, called the Vague or Solar Year, was used concurrently with the Sacred Almanac. The Vague Year had 18 named months of 20 days each (18 x 20 = 360), plus an 'unlucky' period of 5 days added to the year's end to total 365 days. The Maya month names are:

Pohp	Xul	Zak	Pax
Wo	Yaxk'in	Keh	K'ayab
Sip	Mol	Mak	Kumk'u
Sotz'	Ch'en	K'ank'in	Wayeb (the 5-day period)
Sek	Yax	Muwan	

Each day in the month was numbered consecutively, as we number the days of our months. Thus, each day is identified both by its name and number in the Sacred Almanac and by its month name and day number in the Vague Year.

ly. A specific date in the meshed cycles could recur only after 18,980 days, or approximately 52 years, had passed. The end of a 52-year cycle, called a Calendar Round, was a time of important ritual activity.

The Long Count

In addition to these two calendrical cycles, used throughout Mesoamerica, the Maya developed a unique calendrical system that allows us to correlate their calendar with ours. The Long Count recorded 52-year cycle Calendar Round dates within a great cycle of 13 b'aktuns (1,872,000 days, or approximately 5,128 years), thus fixing any given day within the current great cycle. The generally accepted correlation of the Long Count with our calendar places the beginning of the current 5,128-year cycle in August 3114 B.C., and its end in December A.D. 2012.

Days were counted and organized in cumulative blocks of time, thus:

1 k'in = 1 day
1 winal = one 20-day month, or 20 days
1 tun = 18 winals, or 360 days (the single base-20 exception)
1 k'atun = 20 tuns, or 7,200 days
1 b'aktun = 20 k'atuns, or 144,000 days

On the monuments these blocks of time were recorded in reverse fashion, beginning with the number of b'aktuns, ending with the k'ins, and then adding the Calendar Round identification of the day in question.

The use of the Long Count on Maya monuments coincides loosely with the period known as the Maya Classic, A.D. 250–900.

THE MONUMENTS

The Mesoamerican Gallery is graced by some exceptional stone monuments from the Museum's own excavations: Stela 14 and Support 1 of Altar 4 from Piedras Negras; Stelae 16, 6, 17, and 5, and Altars 10 and 13 from Caracol; and Stela 1 from Chocolá (see Figure 1). As it occurs in the ground, limestone is relatively soft, the surface hardening only after exposure. The Maya quarried the native limestone using stone chisels, hammerstones, and, perhaps, wooden mallets. The stone shafts were moved to their destinations probably using tree trunks as rollers, with ropes made from fibrous plants to help haul the heavy load. They were maneuvered into prepared sockets dug into the ground, then pulled upright. Only then did Maya artists carve them with portraits of their kings and inscriptions recording their rulers' great feats.

These monuments are illustrated with line drawings rather than photographs in order to show the detail on the eroded surfaces. The monument descriptions and text paraphrases are by John F. Harris, Research Associate in the American Section. The symbol "(?)" indicates a glyph that has not yet yielded to translation.

Piedras Negras

Piedras Negras was excavated by the University of Pennsylvania Museum from 1931 to 1939. It was the Museum's first major excavation in the Maya region and among the first by any institution in the difficult terrain of the Petén. As part of the Museum's agreement with the Guatemalan government, half of the monuments recovered went to the museum in Guatemala City and half to Philadelphia on long-term loan.

Figure 4. Stela 14, Maya, Piedras Negras, Guatemala, Petén Region. A.D. 758. Limestone. Drawn by John Montgomery.

Only Stela 14 and Support 1 of Altar 4 still remain on loan; the others have been returned to Guatemala.

Piedras Negras was the largest of the Maya sites along the Usumacinta River, and it played an important role in the shifting series of alliances and wars that marked Maya civilization. It also was of great importance to archaeologists more than a millennium after the death of its last king because of a calendar ritual observed by the city's rulers. During the 7th and 8th centuries, sculptured and inscribed monuments were erected to mark each of 22 *hotun* (1,800-day) period endings. All of these monuments survived and led to a remarkable intellectual feat: our understanding of Maya inscriptions.

Stela 14 and its text were part of a breakthrough study in 1960 by Tatiana Proskouriakoff, in which she proved that Maya monumental inscriptions did indeed record historical events. Prior to her work, Maya inscriptions were thought to consist essentially of only calendrical notations and rituals connected with calendrical phenomena. Careful analysis by Proskouriakoff, which began during her work with the Penn team excavating at Piedras Negras in 1936–1937, showed that each of several groups of monuments contained a sequence of dates that were spaced at such intervals that they could correspond to the births, accessions, and deaths of a sequence of rulers. Proskouriakoff's analysis identified the glyphs for events in each ruler's lifetime and pro-

Figure 5. Stela 14 inscription, left side of monument. The text states "on March 14, 758, Black House Great (?) Turtle (Ruler 5) was seated as ruler. He was the child of Divine Lady..."; the inscription ends here. The name phrase for the mother was no doubt continued on the right side of the monument, but severe erosion has completely obliterated the text, and thus we do not know her name. Drawn by John Montgomery.

Figure 6. Scattered throughout the scene on the front of Stela 14 are six small groups of lightly inscribed hieroglyphs. Beginning each group is a hieroglyph whose main sign is the head of a leaf-nose bat, a glyph now interpreted as meaning "his carving," followed by the names or titles of the sculptor who executed the monument. Since there are six such statements on the face of Stela 14, the design and carving of this monument was obviously a multiperson effort. Drawn by John Montgomery.

Figure 7. Altar 4, Maya, Piedras Negras, Guatemala, Petén Region. A.D. 790. Limestone. The inscription along the edge has been almost completely obliterated by erosion, but the Initial Series date of the text has been read as 9.18.0.0.0, 11 Ahaw 18 Mak (October 11, 790), in the reign of the 7th ruler of Piedras Negras.

posed a seven-ruler dynasty for Piedras Negras that is still largely accepted by epigraphers today. Although most subsequent epigraphic research is based on phonetic decipherment unrecognized by Proskouriakoff, her pioneering work was the foundation for the reconstruction of dynastic histories at Tikal, Palenque, Copán, Caracol, and other Maya sites.

Once the inscriptions could be read, this unbroken two-century record provided an extraordinary glimpse into the political history of Piedras Negras. From the 4th century on, the city engaged in particularly fierce conflicts with the neighboring city of Yaxchilan, with each side vying for and trading temporary ascendancy. The last king of Piedras Negras acceded to the throne in 781; his capture in 808 is noted on a Yaxchilan monument erected, ironically, by that city's last ruler. Both cities were abandoned shortly thereafter.

Stela 14 is the finest of the site's unique "niche" sculptures (Figure 4), several of them carved to commemorate the accession of its rulers. It had fallen face down, which probably preserved the carved detail from destruction over the centuries. This monument celebrates the accession of Black House Great (?) Turtle, Ruler 5, whose reign lasted eight years (Figures 5 and 6).

The ruler is portrayed seated on a bench in a niche with his legs crossed and his hands on his knees, wearing an elaborate headdress featuring a Celestial Monster–head mask. Above him is a skyband and the head of a supernatural bird. Leading up to the bench on which the ruler sits is a ladder or scaffold half covered with a

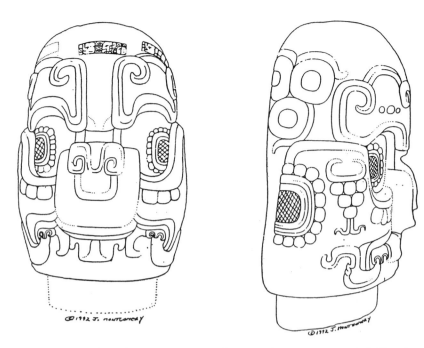

Figure 8. One of the four massive carved stones that once supported Altar 4. Drawn by John Montgomery.

| | Yuxul | Ka'an Ch'ok | Way | |
| | The carving of | Sky Sprout | Spirit Companion | |

Figure 9. The three small horizontal panels of hieroglyphs on the forehead are the signature phrases of the artists who fashioned the stone support for Altar 4. Like the signatures on Piedras Negras Stela 14, each of the texts begins with a glyph that means, "his carving," followed by the names and titles of the artist. Drawn by John Montgomery.

hanging cloth containing footprints suggestive of the ruler's ascent. These crosshatched footprints lead from a badly eroded figure in the lower right corner of the scene—a sacrificed captive whose death was no doubt an important part of the accession ritual. At the left of the scene is a prominently portrayed standing woman, the mother of Ruler 5. Although we know virtually nothing about this woman, she must have been highly important at Piedras Negras to be so pictured. Stela 14 is unique among the niche stelae at Piedras Negras in portraying the mother of the ruler.

Altar 4, an almost square stone slab that probably served as a royal throne (Figure 7), is uncarved on its upper face except for a simple system of channels. The slab remains at the site, but after the University of Pennsylvania's excavations in the 1930s, the four supports were re-

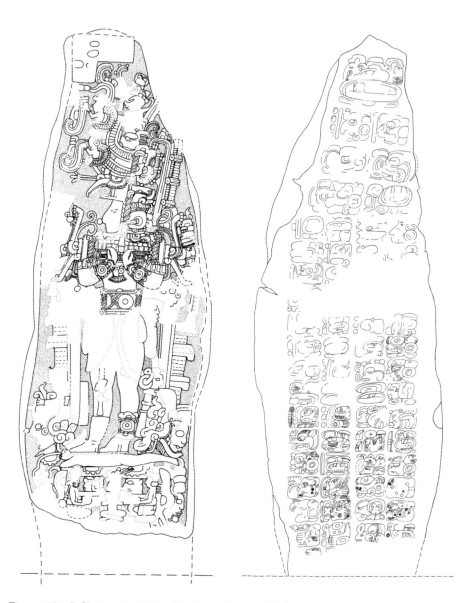

Figure 10a (left). Front of Stela 16, Maya, Caracol, Belize. A.D. 534. Limestone.

Figure 10b. Back of Stela 16. The severely eroded state of the inscription and the unusual glyph forms used make it difficult to interpret the complete text. A partial reading states that K'an I, Ruler 2, ended the 9.5.0.0.0. period (July 5, 534) accompanied by the patron gods of Caracol. On this same day, something was dedicated for Sky Lord, Fire Skull, Sun-Eyed (Ruler 1). K'an I was accompanied by Hun Yoy, Cave Turtle, One (?), the Flint Mountain Lord (Xul Tun Lord). He was the successor of the Divine Scholar Person, Sun-Eyed Jaguar, (?) Cave, Water Lily Jaguar of Copán (Water Lily Jaguar was the 7th ruler of Copán, suggesting a relationship between the two Maya centers that has yet to be understood).
Drawn by Carl Beetz.

moved; Support 1 went to the University of Pennsylvania Museum and the other three to the National Museum in Guatemala City.

Each support represents a grotesque zoomorphic head with very large eyes containing crosshatched ovals surrounded by a circle of dots, a large nose, and upper teeth including curved and pointed canines (Figures 8 and 9). There is no lower jaw. Scrolls abound: scrolls represent the nostrils, there are scroll elements emanating from the corners of the mouth, and there are scrolls on the forehead as continuations of the eyebrows. To the rear of each side is another crosshatched element surrounded by a circle of dots similar to but larger than that in the eye. Near the top of the head to the rear on each side is a triad of circles bordered by snakelike elements. On each cheek is a cluster of balls that has been likened to a bunch of grapes; these hang from an incomplete oval element, and from the grapes hang what is probably a leaf motif. These designs on the sides of the supports are markings characteristic of the heads of the supernatural known as Kawak, a mountain deity, of which the Altar 4 supports may be examples. Kawak markings are also characteristic of many objects made of stone.

Caracol

Caracol lies near the Maya Mountains in south-central Belize. When excavated by the University of Pennsylvania Museum in 1951 and 1953, it was thought to be a relatively unimportant site, peripheral to the major Maya centers. Later excavations have shown that the site is much larger than originally believed, with a very long settlement history, and that it played a crucial role in the political activities of the Maya world. In alliance with Calakmul, one of the most powerful Maya cities, Caracol conducted a series of battles with the great city of Tikal and defeated it in A.D. 562. Caracol in turn was defeated by Tikal in 695. That, and the constantly shifting pattern of alliances, seems to have weakened the Caracol ruling dynasty enough so its rulers were forced to make unusual concessions to their allies. Such is the interpretation of scenes like those on Altar 13 (Figure 14), Stela 17 (Figure 15), and Altar 10 (Figure 16). The last stela erected in the city is dated 859.

Stela 16 is the best preserved of four Early Classic Caracol monuments found buried together in a deposit near the center of the site. The figure on the front of the stela (Figure 10a) is undoubtedly Ruler 2, K'an I, the protagonist of the stela text. The figure holds the two-headed serpent bar and wears a tall headdress with barely discernable human figures. Additional serpent heads on either side of his feet may be the extremities of a sinuous, badly eroded double-headed serpent that once curled around the scene. The text on the back (Figure 10b) is badly eroded and some glyphs have yet to be deciphered, making a complete reading impossible at this time.

Stela 6 is the only Caracol stela that portrays standing figures on both the front and back (Figure 11). The regal figure on the front is believed to be Flaming Ahaw, the ruler who commissioned the stela. He is also shown on Stela 5 (Figure 13). He carries a double-headed serpent bar with heads emerging from the mouths. He wears at least one head on his belt; a dwarf is at his right foot, and he stands on a prone, essentially naked figure, no doubt a soon-to-be sacrificed victim.

The figure on the back (Figure 11, right), also in regal garb, is presumed

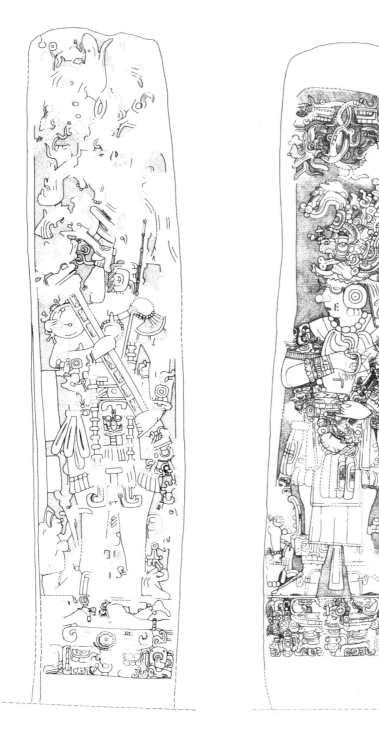

Figure 11. Stela 6, Maya, Caracol, Belize. A.D. 603. Limestone. Front (left) and back of stela. Drawn by Carl Beetz.

Figure 12. The remaining text for Stela 6 records two accession dates and several calendar rituals. It states that on April 18, 553, Lord Water of Caracol (Ruler 3) was seated as ruler, under the supervision of the ruler of Tikal. Following his accession, he celebrated three Period Endings: 9.6.0.0.0 (March 22, 554), 9.7.0.0.0 (December 7, 573), and 9.8.0.0.0. (August 24, 593). After that, the Ahaw headband (rulership) was passed to his son, and on June 26, 599, Flaming Ahaw of Caracol was seated as ruler. Flaming Ahaw (Ruler 4) celebrated the Half Period Ending (9.8.10.0.0, July 4, 603) at the First Five Sky Place of the Paddler Gods, witnessed by the Three K'atun Censor, Lord Water of Caracol. He was accompanied by his younger brother, Na-(?) K'in Chekah of Caracol. Drawn by Carl Beetz.

to be Yahaw Te K'inich (Lord Water), the previous ruler. The bones and bird feathers in his headdress, the curled motif around his eye (a deity marker), and the numeral eight on his cheek (associated with the Maize God, who returns to life each year) are indications that he was deceased when the stela was dedicated. Heads with hieroglyphs in their headdresses project from the mouths of the entwined snakes forming part of the floating motif above the headdress; the glyph above the head on the standing figure's right is the name of Lord Water's predecessor, who may have been his father, (?) Ol K'inich (K'an I).

The inscription on the right side (Figure 12) is especially important since it records that Caracol was subordinate to Tikal at the time of the stela's dedication. Tikal's control was broken a few years later, apparently with the help of Calakmul. The text preserved here represents less than half the hieroglyphs originally carved, which would have included the now-eroded left side of the stela and two small glyph panels on the front.

The image on the front of Stela 5 (Figure 13) is no doubt Flaming Ahaw (Ruler 4) of Caracol. He wears a mon-

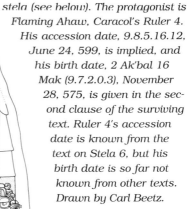

Figure 13. Stela 5, Maya, Caracol, Belize. A.D. 613. Limestone. Only one hieroglyph cartouche remains on the right side of the stela (see below). The protagonist is Flaming Ahaw, Caracol's Ruler 4. His accession date, 9.8.5.16.12, June 24, 599, is implied, and his birth date, 2 Ak'bal 16 Mak (9.7.2.0.3), November 28, 575, is given in the second clause of the surviving text. Ruler 4's accession date is known from the text on Stela 6, but his birth date is so far not known from other texts. Drawn by Carl Beetz.

ster bird headdress above which hover two entwined snakes and a bird, whose heads all disgorge deity or ancestor figures. The ruler holds a double-headed serpent bar from whose heads humans emerge. The costume draping the ruler's body features other heads, and heads on torsos. He stands on a double-headed caiman(?) from whose mouths emerge additional heads. On the ruler's left at his feet stands a dwarf figure; a diminutive normal figure kneels at his right. Behind each of these small figures is a snake head (probably parts of a double-headed snake) with human heads emerging from their mouths. Interestingly, the headdress of the emerging head behind the kneeling figure contains glyphs that read (?) Ol K'inich, the name of the next ruler, Ruler 5, suggesting that the kneeling figure is the heir apparent to Ruler 4.

The costuming of Ruler 4 on Stela 5 is typical of images appearing on many Classic Period stelae from lowland Maya sites. Most of the text on

Figure 14. Altar 13, Maya, Caracol, Belize. A.D. 830. Limestone. The text states that on a date believed to be March 10, 804, an object was displayed or received (probably signaling his accession) by K'inich Tobil Toat (Ruler 10) of Caracol, at the site of Ucanal. He was accompanied by Papamalil of Ucanal. On August 3, 822, Makal Te was decapitated at (?) by Ruler 10 of Caracol accompanied by Papamalil of Ucanal. Drawn by Carl Beetz.

Figure 15. Stela 17, Maya, Caracol, Belize. A.D. 849. Limestone. The text states that on April 18, 849, K'an III, Caracol Ruler 12, formed the earth at the center cave, the Three Mountain Place. On Nov. 30, 849, he performed a scattering ritual, accompanied by his god, Ox (?) Winik. Drawn by Carl Beetz.

the right side of Stela 5 is completely eroded. There were apparently five stacked cartouches of hieroglyphs arranged in a manner similar to those on the left side of Stela 6. Only a portion of the glyphs in the bottom cartouche is readable, and even that not smoothly since some of the elements are missing. Considering the total of the eroded side panels and the now-blank glyph panels on the front, the original text must have numbered well over 200 hieroglyphs.

Altar 13 was discovered in 1951 during the University of Pennsylvania Museum's excavations at Caracol. The two standing figures are identified in the inscription (Figure 14). The more elaborate costuming and posture of the figure on the right identify him as the main authority figure, Caracol Ruler 10. The fourth glyph in the vertical strip of text in back of the figure on the left, although somewhat eroded, is clearly the name Papamalil. Between them is the kneeling figure named as Makal Te.

The main text of the altar, framing the scene, is shaped like a symbolic portal connecting this world with the Other World. There is appreciable erosion of the main text, but much of it can be read. In addition, there are several small groups of glyphs, which have suffered various degrees of erosion. One of these is the T-shaped group located above and between the two standing figures containing a date believed to correspond to March 10, 804. A small enclosed group of glyphs on the

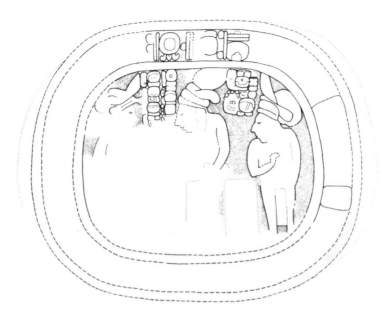

Figure 16. Altar 10, Maya, Caracol, Belize. A.D. 849. Limestone. No co-herent reading or translation of the Altar 10 text is possible at this point because of erosion and damage, but it seems to reproduce at least in part the text on Stela 17. Drawn by Carl Beetz.

left edge of the main text is illegible except for the number 10. A similar grouping on the right of the main text contains the Calendar Round, 7 Ahaw 18 Sip (10.0.0.0.0, March 15, 830), a Period Ending about 20 years before the dedication date of Caracol Stela 17 and Altar 10.

Stela 17 and its companion Altar 10 are among the latest major monuments at Caracol. In fact their dedication date, 10.1.0.0.0 (November 26, 849), is later than the latest dates at many other lowland Classic Maya sites. They were dedicated by the next-to-last known ruler, K'an III (Ruler 12). The scene on Stela 17 (Figure 15) displays a marked departure from previous Caracol stela scenes. Instead of a standing ruler pictured in his regal finery as on

Stelae 5, 6, and 16, and even Altar 13, the Stela 17 scene features two seated figures apparently rather simply costumed. The figures are K'an III, on the left, and K'ak Ahaw Ch'ok (Fire Lord Sprout), a subordinate lord, on the right, with his name above his headdress. Stela 17 and Altar 10 were found near a series of mounds some distance from central Caracol. This peripheral location suggests that they may have been associated with K'ak Ahaw Ch'ok, whose support may have been necessary for Caracol's ruler to maintain control of his kingdom. Such sharing of power is noted at other lowland Maya sites in the final throes of the Classic Period.

The scene on Altar 10 features three individuals (Figure 16), appar-

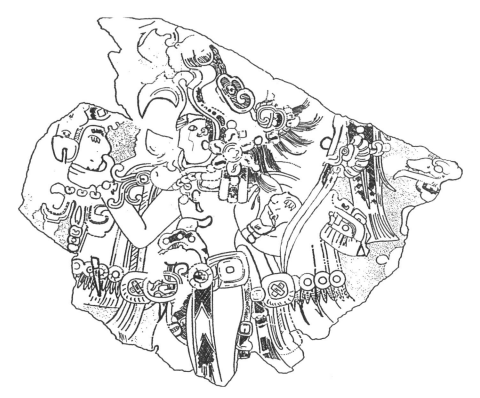

Figure 17. Stela 1, Chocolá, Maya, Guatemala, Pacific Slope. Ca. 300 B.C.–A.D. 300. Porphyritic basalt. The sparsely clothed figure with flowing hair wears a serpent-head helmet, a unique star shape ear ornament, and a masked face on his belt. In his outstretched right hand he holds a helmeted head with its face toward him. In the crook of his left arm is a bearded head with a trefoil eye cover, a motif repeated on Stela 31 of Tikal, carved several centuries later. Some scholars suggest that such heads represent the deified father, and the carving thus imparts legitimacy to the current ruler.

ently all standing, with headdresses resembling those in the scene on Stela 17. Although it is not certain, the middle figure, the largest of the three, probably represents Ruler 12.

Chocolá

In the early years of the 20th century a coffee plantation was located on what was once a Maya site on the Pacific Slope in Guatemala, and periodically the farmers would bring up ancient objects with their plows.

The fragment of Chocolá Stela 1 (Figure 17) was found in such an incident. Although an extensive search was made, this is all that was recovered of what was clearly a much larger monument when first carved. It is a superb example of the flamboyant and highly controlled style of the southern Maya Late Preclassic, which seems to have given inspiration to the early monument carving at Tikal and other lowland Classic Maya sites.

A ROYAL BURIAL

Just as stone monuments glorified Maya rulers, their burials also proclaimed their power and wealth, with offerings that symbolized their prestige and suggest the belief that interment was an interlude leading to an eternal afterlife (Plates 1–5). One example of such a tomb is Burial 5 (Figure 18) at the Maya site of Piedras Negras in Guatemala. In the corbel-vaulted tomb, in addition to the principal figure, the archaeologists found the remains of two children. The vault had collapsed in antiquity, disturbing and damaging most of the furnishings. The tomb is believed to be that of Ruler 3, K'inich Yo'nal Ahk II, who was born on December 29, 664, acceded to the throne on January 2, 687, and ruled for forty-two years. He had fifteen of his teeth drilled and inset with jade and hematite discs; his upper central incisors had been side-notched to imitate the teeth of the Sun God. A small carved jadeite figurine had been placed in his mouth and dozens of jade beads were scattered about the floor; brilliant red pigment adhered to the skeleton and also covered many objects in the grave. Stingray spines (Plate 4), frequently used as bloodletting instruments, were inscribed with his name and placed near his body, along with other offerings of jade (Plates 2, 3), bone (Plate 5), clay, stone, shell, and pyrite.

Four inscribed shell plaques together with other uninscribed shell pieces, all with holes drilled in them, had apparently been sewn on a garment associated with the primary tomb occupant. Only two of four inscribed shell plaques are in the gallery (Plate 1); the other two are in the National Museum in

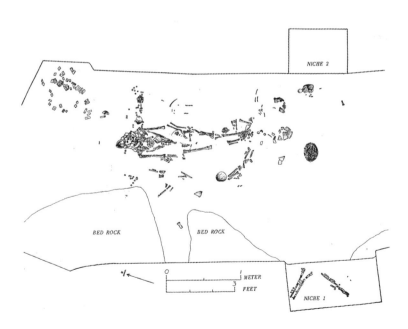

Figure 18. Plan of Burial 5, Piedras Negras.

Figure 19. Shell plaques found in Burial 5, Piedras Negras; translation of their inscriptions follows. The first and third shells are in the National Museum, Guatemala City; the second and fourth are in the University of Pennsylvania Museum.

Shell 1: On 5 Kib 14 Yaxk'in (9.12.2.0.16, July 7, 674) was born Lady Naman Ahaw. Fifteen k'ins, 9 winals...
Shell 2: ...and 12 tuns after that date, dawned 9 Chuwen 9 K'ank'in (9.12.14.10.11, November 16, 686) when Lady Naman Ahaw made a contract (became engaged). God N, the 4 K'atun Lord, the Divine Piedras Negras Lord (Piedras Negras Ruler 2) caused it to be done.
Shell 3: Six days later, on 2 Kaban 15 K'ank'in (9.12.14.10.17, November 22, 686), she (Lady Naman Ahaw) was adorned (married to Ruler 3). She was accompanied by Lady of Bik'al.
Shell 4: Four winals, 3 tuns, and 2 k'atuns later dawned the day 1 Kaban 20 Yaxk'in (9.14.17.14.17, June 30, 729) when Lady Lord of Matawix was adorned (married). Lady Naman Ahaw (wife of Ruler 3) caused it to be done. She was accompanied by Jaguar (?) Turtle, the Piedras Negras Lord, the 4 K'atun Lord, the Sun Lord (Piedras Negras Ruler 3).

Guatemala City. The text is unusual in that it deals almost entirely with women (Figure 19). The main protagonist is Lady Naman Ahaw, whose birth and presumed engagement and marriage to Ruler 3 of Piedras Negras are chronicled in this text. Two other women are mentioned in the text. One is Lady of Bik'al who is said to have accompanied Lady Naman Ahaw at her marriage.

The other woman named in the shell plaques text is Lady Lord of Matawix, whose marriage over twenty years later was brought about by Lady Naman Ahaw. So far she is not known from other texts. We know, from this and other inscriptions at Piedras Negras, that Lady Naman Ahaw was a woman of great importance. In a most unusual honor for a Maya queen, she and her young daughter are the major figures carved on a stela.

THE CULTURES

Following this essay, sixty-four pages of color photographs illustrate the skill of the artisans (Plates 16–38), objects that were used in the home (Plates 6–15), and in rituals (Plates 39–47), including the ritual ball game (Plates 63–67), and they suggest the cultural traditions that motivated the work. The gallery displays artifacts from the following important cultures of Mesoamerica.

Teotihuacán

A huge, carefully planned city with a peak population of as many as 200,000, Teotihuacán covered about 40 square kilometers of a fertile Central Mexico valley, some 40 kilometers northeast of modern Mexico City (Plates 6, 49, 69–71). The city, with its broad avenues and distinctive architectural style, was first laid out between 100 B.C. and A.D. 100, and continued to grow in size and importance for at least five hundred years. Evidence for Teotihuacán's enormous influence throughout Mesoamerica has been found in such far-distant sites as the Maya cities of Tikal in Guatemala and Copán in Honduras. The nature of that influence, whether conquest, trade, or mutual alliances, is still being investigated.

Some time around the middle of the 8th century A.D., the city was destroyed and burned by an as yet unidentified attacker. The fall of Teotihuacán was followed by the rise of the adjacent Toltec culture, with similar cultural elements. Centuries after the city collapsed, burned, and was abandoned, the Aztecs migrated into the region. They offered sacrifices here and gave it the name by which it is known today. In Nahuatl, Teotihuacán means "Birthplace of the Gods." Because none of the original inhabitants' writing has been found, we still do not know the name by which this city was initially known, nor the name the people called themselves.

The Aztecs

The Aztecs, or Mexica, arrived in Central Mexico about A.D. 1250 (Plates 13–15, 17, 18, 72, 73, 76, 95). A semi-nomadic tribe with great military skills, they became mercenaries for one of the local city-states when they first entered the valley. They soon dominated the region, and built their city of Tenochtitlán starting in A.D. 1325. It was a well-protected island city of two-story stone houses, with gardens, well-maintained canals, and both aqueducts and causeways that connected it with the mainland.

Through political acumen, warfare, and control of long-distance trade, the Aztecs became the most important group in Mesoamerica until the Spanish Conquest. Surviving tribute lists show an amazing variety and quantity of goods provided to the Aztecs from the farthest reaches of Mesoamerica. Their use of human sacrifice in their religious rituals is well known. They were also poets, architects, artists, and philosophers.

The Zapotecs and Mixtecs

Over the centuries, two neighboring peoples—the Zapotecs and the Mixtecs—made their home in the Oaxaca Valley in south-central Mexico (Plates 29, 30, 81–87).

By around 500 B.C., the Zapotecs began building the city of Monte Albán, which functioned as both ceremonial center and political capital of the region. Evidence shows they irrigated and terraced the surrounding mountainsides for farming and residential areas, constructed a major ceremonial center with large pyramids, and developed a writing system and a calendar. Long-distance traders carried their wares throughout Meso-america; an area of Teotihuacán seems to have been set aside as a Oaxacan enclave. The hierarchy of Monte Albán collapsed in the political unrest that marked the end of the Classic Period throughout Mesoamerica, around A.D. 700, and was replaced with a series of small city-states.

In the 10th century, the Mixtecs, whose small kingdoms were loosely connected to each other by royal marriages, intermarried with the Zapotecs, and for a time became the primary culture in the Oaxaca Valley.

Gulf Coast Cultures

Several different groups shared this rich region. Among the earliest Meso-american cultures was that of the Olmec (Plates 32–34, 40, 41), with major centers along the Gulf Coast from 1200 to 300 B.C. Evidence of their influence has been found as far away as El Salvador (Plate 34) and Central Mexico. The Olmec built large earthen pyramids, carved huge boulders into portraits of their rulers, and created the beginnings of a calendar and a writing system. Their artistry is nowhere more evident than in the portable objects of stone, pottery, and jade found through-out their sphere of influence.

In northern reaches of the Gulf Coast lived the Huastec, who spoke a form of Mayan and are believed to have become separated from the rest of Mayan-speaking peoples about 1500 B.C. The central region of the Gulf Coast saw the rise of the cultures of Remojadas (A.D. 500–700) and El Tajín (A.D. 600–1100). Much of their art reflects the great ritual importance of the Mesoamerican ball game (Plates 63–67) in the region.

West Mexico Cultures

The role of western Mexico in the complex history of Mesoamerica is just beginning to be known through scientific excavation. The cultures are among those about which little is known, since most artifacts have been found not by archaeological ex-cavation but by large-scale and long-term looting. This perhaps began with the Aztecs in the 14th century and continues to the present time with ever-greater damage to our ability to understand the past.

In the Late Preclassic and Early Classic eras (A.D. 150–500), the cultures around the modern states of Colima and Nayarit buried their dead in shaft tombs in which large and small pottery effigy figures and hollow vessels were found (Plates 39, 52, 77, 89). Their purpose is unknown, but recent interpretations suggest sha-manic ritual. Dogs were believed to conduct their masters' souls to the land of the dead (Plate 79). Recent re-search suggests the possibility of coastal sea trade with Peru, based on the similarity of stirrup-handled pot-tery styles and shaft graves, and the development of sophisticated metal-lurgy.

Guerrero was rich in a variety of minerals, including serpentine, jadeite, andesite, amethyst, garnet, alabaster, and other stones (Plates 45, 52, 78, 80). These raw materials and the region's talented sculptors helped it become a major production center of Teotihuacán-style stone masks. Unfortunately, most of the objects from Guerrero have come from unscientific excavations and their dating is questionable.

The Maya

The Pacific coastal plain and high-lands of Guatemala were important parts of the long-distance trade net-works that extended from the coast of the Gulf of Mexico south to El Salva-dor and beyond. These trade routes began as early as 1500 B.C.; by 400 B.C. Kaminaljuyu in the Valley of Guatemala was the largest and most powerful highland site in the southern region. Because of its location next to Guatemala City, much of the ancient site has been destroyed or covered over by the encroaching development of the modern city.

During a short period in the Late Classic (ca. A.D. 650–750), Chamá, a site in the Alta Verapaz region of Guatemala, produced a type of painted pottery cylinders reminiscent of the Classic Maya painting styles of the lowlands (Plates 98, 102). These vessels provide one of the many forms of evidence for continued interregional interaction.

From A.D. 250 to 900, Maya civilization was centered in the lowland rain forests. At its peak the Maya lowlands supported several million people fed by diverse farming methods, terracing and raised garden beds, orchards of tropical fruits, and slash-and-burn agriculture in marginal areas. Warfare between towns was apparently common, but diplomacy and marital alliances served to create cooperation in trade and war.

At the beginning of the 9th century, the southern lowland cities entered a period of rapid decline. The last inscribed monument with a Long Count date was erected at the site of Toniná in A.D. 909, and most of the lowland cities were abandoned by the middle of the 10th century. But Maya civilization did not disappear.

The decline of the southern lowland cities allowed other centers to become more important. In northern Yucatán, Chichén Itzá, Uxmal, Mayapan, and Tulum began their rise to power after A.D. 900; in the centuries before the Conquest, the Quiché kingdoms were all-powerful in the highlands of Guatemala.

The Southeastern Borderlands

The lands bordering the Maya region influenced and were influenced by their neighbors to both north and south through trade along routes that had been established for more than a millennium (Plates 103–108). Archaeological evidence reveals that the different groups in this intermediate area excelled in relatively small-scale stone sculpture, jadework, and ceramics.

In the Ulúa Valley of Honduras, craftsmen developed a particularly beautiful and unusual tradition of carved marble vases that were traded widely (Plates 104–107). The people of this region were not Maya, but were strongly influenced by Maya culture and symbolism and incorporated Maya iconography in their art.

The Conquest and After

When the Spaniards arrived in the 16th century, Mesoamerica was divided into the Maya area to the east and the Aztec-dominated area to the west. The Aztecs had not conquered the Maya, but they depended heavily upon Maya trade to provide them with the luxury goods—chocolate, cotton, tropical feathers, and jade—which helped to bind together the powerful states. This economic interdependence between east and west can be traced back to the Formative Period, and was especially evident in the Classic Period, when Maya centers such as Tikal in the Guatemalan lowlands flourished in the east and the much larger site of Teotihuacán near modern Mexico City prospered in the west.

In the years immediately following the Conquest, the people of Mesoamerica were decimated by war and disease. The cities of the Aztecs and the Maya were torn down and European-style buildings rose in their stead; churches and monastaries were built on top of the Precolumbian temples. Indigenous religion, writing, and art were suppressed. Nonetheless, there were a few priests and friars who attempted to record, through personal observation and the words of native informants, as much of the Precolumbian culture as they could gather. These early accounts have been of great importance in later attempts to piece together the history of Preconquest Mesoamerica.

Precolumbian culture survived, and, despite five hundred years of European influence, many of the more isolated regions continue to observe the ancient traditions and speak their ancestral languages. Daykeepers in the Maya highlands maintain the 260-day calendar; rain ceremonies are still performed. Maya farmers prepare their cornfields with age-old and unchanging ritual. Textiles woven by the Maya today (Plates 10–12) have a well-deserved reputation for beauty. As in centuries past, the textiles of 20th–century highland Guatemala continue to weave unchanging patterns into the fabric of traditional Maya garb.

A sampling of the richness and variety of Mesoamerican cultures can be found in the painted pottery, figurines, and sculptures in the Mesoamerican Gallery and in the photographs in this guide.

Suggested Reading

Readers who would like to continue their exploration of ancient Mesoamerica may find the following publications to be helpful.

Fash, William. *Scribes, Warriors and Kings: The City of Copán and the Ancient Maya.* Rev. ed. London: Thames & Hudson, 2001.

Harris, John F., and Stephen K. Stearns. *Understanding Maya Inscriptions: A Hieroglyphic Handbook.* 2nd rev. ed. Philadelphia: University of Pennsylvania Museum of Archaeology and Anthropology, 1997.

Harrison, Peter D. *The Lords of Tikal: Rulers of an Ancient Maya City.* London: Thames & Hudson, 1999.

Martin, Simon, and Nikolai Grube. *Chronicle of the Maya Kings and Queens: Deciphering the Dynasties of the Ancient Maya.* London: Thames & Hudson, 2000.

Miller, Mary, and Karl Taube. *The Gods and Symbols of Ancient Mexico and the Maya: An Illustrated Dictionary of Mesoamerican Religion.* New York: Thames & Hudson, 1993.

Sabloff, Jeremy A. *The Cities of Ancient Mexico: Reconstructing a Lost World.* London: Thames & Hudson, 1989.

———. *The New Archaeology and the Ancient Maya.* New York: Scientific American Library, 1990.

Sharer, Robert J. *The Ancient Maya.* 5th ed. Stanford, CA: Stanford University Press, 1994.

Weaver, Muriel Porter. *The Aztecs, Maya, and Their Predecessors: Archaeology of Mesoamerica.* 3rd ed. San Diego: Academic Press, 1993.

About the Author

Elin Danien became an archaeologist after careers in the theater and in advertising. She earned her doctorate in 1998, with a dissertation on "Chama Polychrome Ceramic Cylinders in the University of Pennsylvania Museum." Currently a Research Associate in the American Section of the University of Pennsylvania Museum of Archaeology and Anthropology, as the Museum's first Public Programs Coordinator she originated and for many years ran the Museum's renowned annual Maya Weekend. The volume *New Theories on the Ancient Maya* which she edited with Robert J. Sharer was based on papers given at the 1987 Maya Weekend. Her research interests include the history of archaeology, and she is currently working on a biography of Robert Burkitt, an archaeologist famous in Guatemalan circles as the man who came to tea and stayed for thirty years. In 1986 she established the Bread Upon the Waters scholarship for women over the age of thirty who can pursue an undergraduate degree at the University of Pennsylvania only as part-time students. To date, thirty-five "Bread" scholars have graduated, twenty with honors; another thirty are currently taking courses.

Index

flute **45, 46**
frogs **7, 43**

Gordon, George Byron 1
Grant, Lynn xv
Greater Nicoya Region **28**
Greene, Virginia xv
greenstone **33, 34, 45, 64, 71, 103**
grinding stone (metate) xii, **8**
Guatemala 1, **10, 11, 12, 13, 16, 35,
36, 37, 40, 42, 43, 46, 47, 49, 55,
57, 65**
    highlands 4, 22, 23, **10, 16**
    lowlands xiii, 23, **107**
    Pacific coastal plain xii, 22, **97**
    Petén 1, 5, 8
Guatemala City, Guatemala 5, 23
    National Museum xiii, 5, 19
Guerrero, Mexico 22, **45, 52, 54, 58, 78**
Gulf Coast, Mexico 22, **51, 64, 65, 66,
91**
    El Tajin 22
    Olmec 22
    Remojadas 22, **67, 91, 92, 93, 94**

hachas **65**
Harris, John F. xv, 3, 5
headdress 8, 11, 13, 15, 18, **34, 36,
52, 62, 81, 82, 90, 91, 93, 99**
Hero Twins **16, 63**
hieroglyphic inscriptions (Maya) 3
    glyph elements 3
        affixes 3
        main sign 3
    reading order 3
Honduras 1, **104**
    Ulua Valley 23, **104, 105, 106, 107,
108**
Huastec 22
Huehuetenango, Guatemala **47**
human sacrifice 9, 11, 21, **47**

incense burner **15, 68**

jade and jadeite 19, 22, 23, **2, 3, 32,
33, 37, 38, 40, 55, 57, 60, 85, 86,
103**
jaguar **3, 5, 8, 38, 40, 41, 59, 62, 98,
102, 106**
Jalisco, Mexico **56**
jewelry **2, 18, 21, 22, 30, 34, 35, 36,
37, 38, 48, 49, 53, 54, 55, 56, 57,
77, 88, 91, 96, 99, 103**
Jones, Christopher xv

K'ak Ahaw Ch'ok (Fire Lord Sprout). See
    Caracol
Kaminaljuyu, Guatemala 23
K'an I (Ruler 2, Ol K'inich). See Caracol
K'an III (Ruler 12). See Caracol
K'inich Tobil Toat (Ruler 10). See
    Caracol
Kline, Charles xv
Kyle, Elena xiv, xv

labret **26, 53**
Lamp, Kevin xv
leaf-nose bat 7, **92, 104**
limestone 5, 6, 8, 10, 12, 14, 15, 16,
    17, **59, 61, 65, 100**
Long-nosed God **62, 96**
looting 2
Lord Water of Caracol. See Caracol
lost-wax technique **27, 30**

Maize God 13, **62**
marble vessels **104, 105, 106, 107**
mask/maskette **71, 78, 90, 92, 93, 94**
Mason, J. Alden xiii, 1
Matawix, Lady Lord of. See Piedras
    Negras
mat design **3B, 104**
Maya xiii, 21, **1, 2, 3, 4, 5, 10, 11, 12,
13, 16, 23, 24, 35, 36, 37, 40, 42,
43, 46, 47, 48, 49, 55, 57, 58, 59,
60, 61, 62, 63, 65, 92, 96, 97, 98,
99, 100, 102, 104, 105, 107, 108**
Maya arithmetic 3, Figure 3
    base-20 system 3
    deity-head glyphs 3
    symbols 3, Figure 3
        bar 3
        dot 3
        shell 3
Maya calendar system 4
    Long Count 3, 5, **47**
    Sacred Almanac 4
    Vague or Solar Year 4
Maya Classic period xiii, 5, 15, 17, 18,
23
    painting styles 23
Maya Early Classic period 22
Maya Late Classic period 23, **98**
Maya Late Preclassic period 18, 22
Maya Preclassic period 22
Maya writing 3, Figure 2
    hieroglyphs 3
metallurgy **27, 28, 29, 30, 31**
Metcalf, Walda xv

PLATE 1

Inscribed spondylus shell plaques
Maya, Piedras Negras, Guatemala, Burial 5. 8th century.
Left: H. 6.6 cm; W. 8.5 cm. Right: H: 7.3 cm; W: 4.2 cm
L-27-41; L-27-42

The text tells us that on July 7, 674, Lady Naman Ahaw was born, on November 16, 686, she became engaged, and six days later she was married to Ruler 3 of Piedras Negras; on June 20, 729, Lady K'atun Ahaw and her husband arranged the marriage of Lady Lord of Matawix. (See drawing of inscription on p. 20, Figure 19.)

PLATE 2

Rectangular jadeite bead
Maya, Piedras Negras, Guatemala, Burial 5. 8th century. L. 10 cm
L-27-21

This bead still bears traces of red color on three sides. Each end is decorated by double bands in relief and a flower-like design. Found in the area of the ruler's chest.

PLATE 3A

Jadeite relief carving
Maya, Piedras Negras, Guatemala,
Burial 5. 8th century. L: 8.2 cm
L-27-19

Found partially under the vertebrae
of the ruler, this carving was bored in
several places from side to back, suggesting that it may have been sewn to
a garment. The jaguar's ear is slightly
broken.

PLATE 3B

The inscription on the back of
the carving is fragmentary. The
upper glyphs can be read as
"Mountain Lord." In the lower
line the last two glyphs on the
right are the Venus sign and the
mat sign, usually indicative of
rulership or the throne.

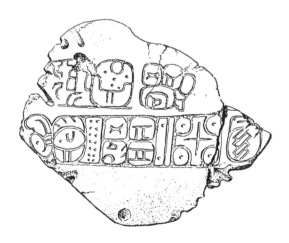

PLATE 4
Stingray spines
Maya, Piedras Negras, Guatemala, Burial 5. 8th century. Dimension of largest ca. 5.5 cm
L-27-46

Four complete stingray spines, shattered into ten fragments, were inscribed with the name of K'inich Yo'nal Ahk II; they were found near Ruler 3's right elbow.

PLATE 5
Carved bone
Maya, Piedras Negras, Guatemala, Burial 5. 8th century. H. 9.5 cm
L-27-45

A bird figure carved from a jaguar ulna, found near the ruler's right arm. This may represent the Muan bird, the screech owl associated with rain, maize, and the Underworld.

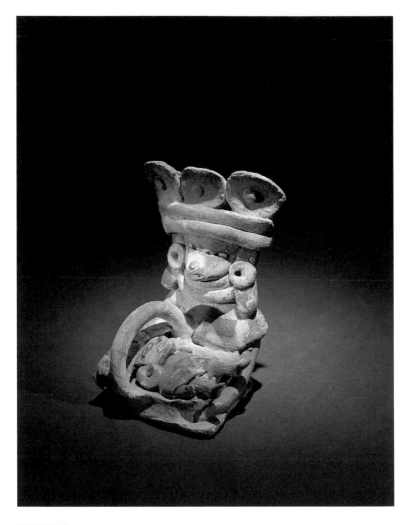

PLATE 6

Pottery figurine, seated female with infant
Teotihuacán, Central Mexico. Ca. A.D. 200. H. 11 cm
66-30-18

Figurines are abundant in Central Mexican sites. Some can offer a glimpse
of everyday life, as in this view of a mother and infant. Note the cradle-
board used to flatten the infant's forehead.

PLATE 7
Obsidian frog
Aztec?, Mexico. A.D. 1325–1519. L. 10 cm; W. 7.5 cm
L-83-186

In addition to its legendary and mythic aspects, the frog was considered to be a healthful food. It was used as a medicinal ingredient and continued to have such purposes among traditional Maya in the early years of the 20th century.

PLATE 8
Grinding stone
Guanacaste, Costa Rica. A.D. 900–1200? H. 9 cm; L. 31.8 cm
39-29-3

Stones like this were used to grind maize, nuts, and seeds. A long, rounded hand stone (*mano*) completes this implement (see p. xii for another grinding stone with *mano*). The carved animal may be a jaguar.

PLATE 9
Pottery whistle in the form of a seated female
Central Veracruz, Mexico. Ca. A.D. 800. H. 11.5 cm
69-24-1

Although clothing does not usually survive, ancient figurines such as this provide tantalizing hints of the intricate weaves and embroidered patterns of
ancient textiles.

PLATE 10

Ball of brown cotton yarn. Maya, Guatemala highlands. 20th century
Raw brown cotton. Maya, Guatemala highlands. 20th century
Dried thistle (carder). Maya, Guatemala highlands. 20th century
Wooden spindle and discoid whorl, with cotton thread. Maya. 20th century
42-35-446; 42-325-295; 42-35-143; 42-35-246

This photograph shows some of the ingredients used in the preparation of cloth. To loosen the fibers after harvesting, the natural brown raw cotton is beaten with wooden sticks on packed dried cornhusks covered with deerskin. Carders such as this thistle are used to disentangle the fibers to prepare them for spinning with a spindle, the end of which usually rests in a clay dish, gourd, or seashell, or on the ground. The weaver, traditionally a woman, has a supply of the raw cotton over her shoulder or in a small basket. After spinning, the thread is wound into a ball, ready for weaving.

PLATE 11

Purpura shell. Coast of Corinto, Nicaragua. 20th century. H. 7 cm
Cotton yarn. Maya, Guatemala. 20th century
42-35-452; 42-35-451

Collected in the 1930s, this cotton yarn was dyed with the extract from the *Purpura* mollusc; today, aniline dyes replace the rare and expensive extract.

PLATE 12

Cotton and wood doll
Maya, Guatemala. Early 20th century. H. 10.2 cm; L. 13.6. cm
67-31-02

This doll illustrates the traditional position of weaver, backstrap loom, and post. Note the ball of yarn at the side of the loom.

PLATE 13

Alabaster effigy vases
Left: Maya, Esquintla, Guatemala. Ca. A.D. 1000–1500. H. 16.5 cm. Right: Aztec, Mexico. 1325–1519. H. 13.5 cm 12681; NA6362

Monkeys are depicted in Maya art as scribes and as patron gods of art, writing, and calculating. The spider monkey was identified with licen-

tiousness and sexual abandon, an apt symbol for these vases, which would have held a beverage made from ground cacao beans, illustrated here. This frothy chocolate drink was believed to have aphrodisiac qualities.

PLATE 14

Tripod pottery bowl
Aztec, Valley of Mexico.
A.D. 1425–1450.
H. 9 cm; Dia. 21.5 cm
29-166-21

A bowl such as this, for grating chile, would have been found in every Aztec kitchen. Chile was roasted on a griddle, eaten plain as a relish, simmered in stews, rubbed on meats, and sometimes added to the beverage made from cacao beans. For additional 'fire,' the seeds would be included in the cookpot.

PLATE 15

Pottery incense bowl, rosette applique, twisted tripod supports
Aztec, Central Mexico.
A.D. 1400–1519. H. 9.5 cm
L-83-209

Ancient incense bowls ranged in size from a few inches to several feet in height. The aromatic resin called *pom* (Mayan) or *copalli* (Nahuatl) is burned today as it was in Precolumbian times, both in the home and as part of ritual.

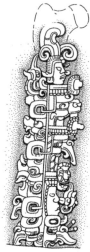

PLATE 16A

Carved animal bones
Maya, Guatemala. A.D. 400. L. 21.5 cm; L. 18.5 cm; L. 21 cm
68-32-2a; 68-32-3; 68-32-2b

These bones, carved in the Early Classic style of Tikal in Guatemala, were found in a tomb in Michoacan, western Mexico. Why they were carried over 500 miles, and who the tomb's inhabitant was, is unknown.

PLATE 16B

Drawing of the designs carved into two of the bones. They seem to be a pair celebrating the mythic Hero Twins, important figures in the *Popol Vuh,* the creation myth of the highland Maya. The figure on 68-32-3 in Plate 16A may represent a Maya lord.

PLATE 17

Obsidian points
Aztec?, Mexico. A.D. 1325–1519
Clockwise from top: L. 5.6 cm; L. 4.8 cm; L. 7.4 cm; L. 6.9 cm; L. 5.6 cm
11261; 11253; 11244; 11242; 11246

When volcanic lava with a high silica content cools quickly, it produces obsidian, a hard natural glass. Its ability to hold a very sharp cutting edge made obsidian an extremely valuable material.

PLATE 18

Red-veined obsidian
Aztec?, Mexico. A.D. 1325–1519.
L. 3.2 cm; H. 1.8 cm
NA5974

In addition to weapons and cutting tools, obsidian was used for ear plugs, pendants such as this dog head, and other decorative adornments.

PLATE 19

Copal resin figurine
Sitio Conte, Cocle, Panama. A.D. 900–1500. H. 5 cm; L. 8 cm
40-13-605

Resins were used as incense and also, as in this charming figure, as a sculptural medium. While fresh and pliable, resin was formed into this little toucan. It was found during the University of Pennsylvania Museum excavation of Sitio Conte in 1940.

PLATE 20

Fluted alabaster jar
Aztec?, Mexico. A.D. 1325–1519.
H. 16.2 cm; Dia. 10 cm
L-83-203

The translucent qualities of alabaster and its relative ease of carving made it a desirable material for bowls and small statues. The low-relief fluting on the nearly cylindrical sides of this vase suggests petals; the vessel body sits on three ball feet.

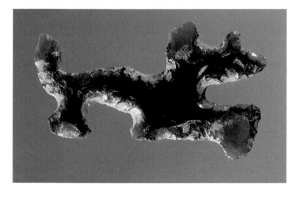

PLATE 21

Obsidian dog. Aztec?
Mexico. A.D. 1325–1519. L. 3.1 cm
Stone claw pendant
Mixteca Alta, Oaxaca, Mexico. A.D. 700–1100. H. 2.7 cm
CG 2001-2-10; 29-41-1033

Iron and magnesium give the obsidian a dark green to black color. This translucent scrap, probably the detritus of a larger carving, was turned into a miniature masterpiece by an unknown artist. The thin sliver of stone, shaped by a superb craftsman, was deposited as part of the tomb furnishings of a Mixtec lord.

PLATE 22

Top: Oval stone bead. Mixtec, Mixteca Alta, Oaxaca, Mexico. A.D. 700–1100. L. 4.4 cm
Left: Reddish translucent stone pendant. Aztec?, Mexico. A.D. 1300–1519. L. 4.5 cm
Bottom right: Dark green stone pendant. Mixtec, Mixteca Alta, Oaxaca, Mexico.
A.D. 700–1100. L. 4.5 cm
29-41-1038; NA5981; 29-41-986

Stone for beads and pendants was selected on the basis of color, then shaped by chipping, sawing, and grinding, with polishing as the final step in the process.

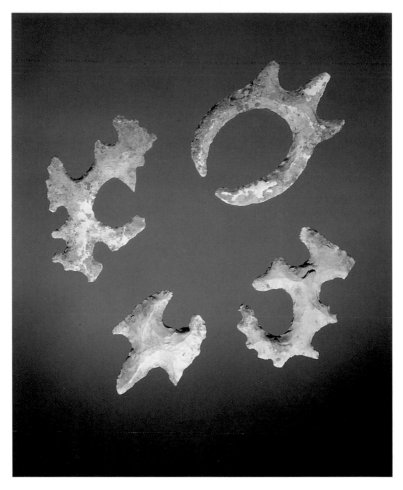

PLATE 23
Eccentric flints
Maya, Piedras Negras, Guatemala. 8th century A.D. Clockwise from top:
L. 7.8 cm; L. 6.3 cm; L. 5.1 cm; L. 7.8 cm
L-16-309-l; L-16-309-g; L-16-309-m; L-16-309-i

These eccentrics are from various caches at the site of Piedras Negras. Cache materials include flint, obsidian, jade, and shell. Shapes and designs include faces, deities, insects, reptilians, and other animals.

PLATE 24

Eccentric flints
Maya, Guatemala, Piedras Negras. 8th century A.D.
Clockwise, from bottom: L. 17.4 cm; Dia. 7.3 cm; L. 13 cm; L. 9.5 cm; L. 15.2 cm
L-16-309-c; L-16-309-d; L-88-495-b; L-39-116-b; L-39-116-a

Offertory caches were used in dedication and termination rituals, placed
beneath buildings and stelae, at the corners of stairways, and in tombs. Objects
were placed in covered bowls, or enclosed in lip-to-lip dishes.

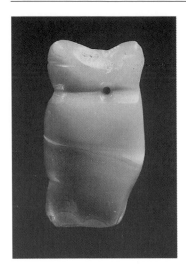

PLATE 25
Amber-colored stone pendant
Chorotegan?, Costa Rica. A.D. 1000–1400. H. 5.3 cm
47-9-8

This highly polished, translucent stone is carved to high-
light its two lobes and veining.

PLATE 26
Clockwise from left: Faceted rock crystal bead. Aztec?, Mexico. A.D. 1325–1519. L. 4 cm.
Rock crystal bead. Aztec, Mexico. A.D. 1325–1519. Dia. 1.9 cm.
Smoky quartz pendant, duck's head. Aztec?, Mexico. A.D. 1325–1519. L. 4.6 cm.
Rock crystal labret: Aztec, Mexico. A.D. 1325–1519. H. 1.5 cm.
Green and white agate pendant, bird's head. Aztec?, Mexico. A.D. 1325–1519. L. 2.5 cm
NA5989; NA5978; NA5976; CG2001-2-11; NA5975

The ritual importance of agate, rock crystal, and other quartz formations lives on in
many parts of Mesoamerica, perhaps because their transparent and translucent qualities
seem to provide the ability to "see" into another dimension. The labret was shaped to
fit through a small hole made in the lower lip, the flat back anchoring it.

PLATE 27

Copper bells
Mexico. A.D. 900–1519. L. 5 cm; L. 5.2 cm
NA5885; NA5886

Well-developed copper metallurgy first appeared in western and north-western Mexico shortly before A.D. 800. Bells were cast using the lost-wax method and were traded widely throughout Mesoamerica. Although metals were produced in West Mexico, the style and workmanship of many of the items found in the Maya region and the Valley of Mexico suggest they were made in Central America and imported.

PLATE 28

Copper bell
Central America, Greater Nicoya Region. A.D. 900–1520. L. 5.2 cm
51-46-202

Mesoamerican metallurgy design characteristics and fabrication techniques may have been derived from lower Central America and from Ecuador and Colombia in South America.

PLATE 29

Cast copper blade
Zapotec, Oaxaca, Mexico. A.D. 800–1200. L. 15.7 cm; W. of blade: 16.5 cm
29-41-939

Copper blades like this are found in tombs, usually grouped in a circle with the handles
turned to the center. Craftsmen used open-mold casting, cold work, and then annealing.

PLATE 30

Copper ring
Mixtec, Mexico. A.D. 1000–1200. Design H. 2 cm
L-144-3

The bird's head design on this finger ring was
made using the lost-wax technique. One of many
objects collected in the early 19th century by the
Honorable Joel R. Poinsett, first U.S. Minister to
Mexico, a role he filled from 1825 to 1829.

PLATE 31

Textile fragment, cotton lace, string, snail shells, and copper bells
Nayarit, Mexico. A.D. 1000–1519. L. 9.4 cm
NA6357

With the advent of metallurgy, tiny bells were added to snail shells as
decorative features on Mesoamerican clothing. Salts from the metal
corrosion of the tiny bells on this fragment impregnated the cloth and
helped preserve it.

PLATE 32

Jadeite heads
Olmec, Mexico. 600–300 B.C. H. 3.2 cm; H. 4.3 cm; H. 2.5 cm
NA5919; NA5917; NA5918

Jadeite has been considered a prestige material in Mesoamerica for 3,000 years. It was carved in sizes from miniatures of less than an inch to a massive sculpted boulder weighing almost ten pounds. The Olmec preferred the lustrous bluegreen jadeite believed to have come from Costa Rica.

PLATE 33

Greenstone (probably jadeite) figurines
Olmec, Mexico. 600–300 B.C. H. 14.5 cm; H. 11.3 cm
63-18-1; NA5913

Mesoamerican artisans used cords covered with resin and stone particles as saws and sharpened hardwood or bone as drills, in each case with quartz sand and crushed jade as the abrasive agent.

PLATE 34

Polished greenstone pendant
Olmec, Central America. 900–300 B.C. H. 6.3 cm
NA5906

Olmec artists brought a sense of monumentality to even the smallest of their carvings. This seated figure wears what appears to be a mask over his left eye, a knobbed pillbox headdress, and wide belt.

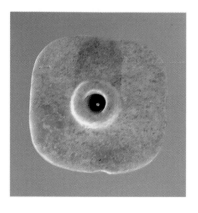
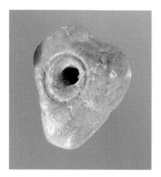

PLATE 35

Jadeite earflare, traces of red paint on white lime
Maya, Piedras Negras, Guatemala, Burial 5. 8th century. 6 cm by 6 cm
Jadeite pebble
Chorotegan?, Costa Rica. A.D. 800–1200. L. 4.2 cm by 3.2 cm
L-27-35; 47-9-10

Jade was associated with maize, water, sky, and vegetation. A jade pebble was sometimes placed in the mouth of the dead as a sign of the renewal of life. The partially worked apple-green triangular jade pebble reveals tool marks that would have been smoothed away in a final polishing.

PLATE 36

Jadeite pendants
Maya, Guatemala?
A.D. 600–900.
Left: H. 5.7 cm;
Right: H. 5.5 cm
NA5897; NA5900

Found in Mexico, these Maya-style reliefs were perhaps acquired in trade. Their individuality suggests that they are true portraits of elite personages. Plaques depicting Maya lords are found throughout the Maya region, in elite tombs and as offerings at pilgrimage sites. The lords wear earplugs and necklaces. The figure in the pendant on the left has a bird in his headdress; the other figure wears a carving of a bird as the central element of his necklace.

PLATE 37

Jadeite pendant
Maya, Guatemala. A.D. 600–800. H. 2.5
cm; Dia. 3.3 cm
37-13-85

This polished gray-green stone has four
protuberances with depressed centers
on its sides.

PLATE 38

Jadeite pendant
Mixtec, Oaxaca, Mexico.
A.D. 700–1100.
H. 2.2 cm; W. 3.5 cm
5955

Mixtec artisans were famed
for their intricate miniature
carvings, as in this small pen-
dant with the face of the Central Mexican rain god Tlaloc on one
side and the open maw and fangs of a jaguar on the reverse.

PLATE 39

Pottery figurines
Colima, Mexico. A.D. 100–400. Shaman with horn: H. 13.8 cm.
Two shamans wrestling: H. 6.7 cm
60-7-20; 66-30-20

Shamans communicated directly with the supernatural, sometimes achieving trance with the help of hallucinogens, sometimes seeming to transform themselves into the gods or their animal counterparts. They were frequently depicted as horned.

PLATE 40

Jadeite *were-jaguar* mask
Olmec, Mexico.
900–300 B.C. H. 9.3 cm
Pottery whistle figurine,
shaman in transformation
Maya, Chamá, Alta Verapaz, Guatemala. A.D. 700–900. H. 12.5 cm
NA5904; NA11208

The Olmec *were-jaguar* is believed to be one of the earliest manifestations of the jaguar as deity, representing the child born of the union of human and jaguar. Transformation figurines reflect the Mesoamerican belief in the ability of shamans to shift forms.

PLATE 41

Stone figurine
Olmec, Gulf Coast, Mexico.
900–300 B.C. H. 7 cm
31-25-4

Another view of the *were-jaguar*, this one with downward curling jaguar mouth and human body.

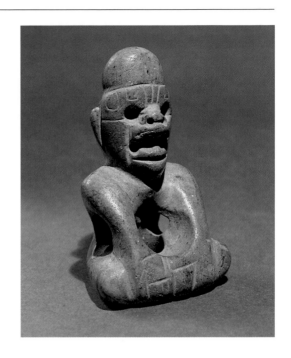

PLATE 42

Pyrite mosaic mirrors
Maya, Kixpek, Guatemala. A.D. 1000–1200. From left: Dia. 10.7 cm; 12 cm square
NA11611; NA11610

Because they seem to capture images and provide a window into the Other World, mirrors are believed to have been part of the shaman's toolkit. When polished, these mosaic mirrors would have dazzled onlookers with reflected sun or firelight.

PLATE 43

Pottery effigy bowl
Maya. Said to be from Chalchuapa, El Salvador, or Asuncion Mita,
Guatemala. Ca. 300 B.C.–A.D. 300. H. 12.5 cm; L. 31.5 cm; W. 26.3 cm
37-13-165

For more than 3,000 years, frogs and toads have played an important role
in Mesoamerican ceremonies. Glands of the *Bufo marinus*, the marine toad,
provided mind-altering substances that helped shamans commune with the
gods through trance states. In traditions that continue into the present day,
young boys mimic frog calls during rain ceremonies to induce rain.

PLATE 44

Pottery rattle
Mixtec, Oaxaca, Mexico. A.D. 900–1200.
H. 10.8 cm
29-41-600

The head is probably that of the Old God, a
guardian of hearth and household. In use,
colorful feathers anchored in the holes in
the head would have added their movement
to the sound of clay pellets as dancers used
the rattle to keep time.

PLATE 45

Greenstone carving of a flute player
Guerrero?, Mexico. 300 B.C.–A.D. 500.
H. 7.7 cm
NA5916

Throughout Mesoamerica, music has
an important role in all ritual. Ritual
ceremonies accompanied by drum,
flute, and whistle can be seen today
among those who still follow the
ancient traditions, and modern per-
formers are very like the musician in
this carving.

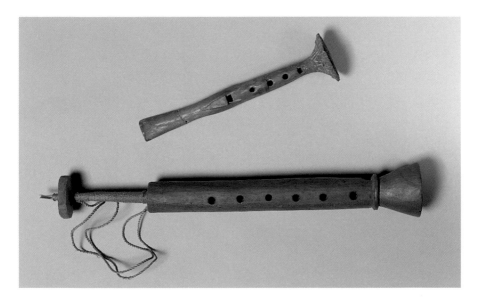

PLATE 46

Pottery flute. Aztec, Central Mexico. A.D. 1400–1519. L. 22.86 cm
Wood, reed and string flute. Maya, Guatemala. Early 20th century. L. 41.6 cm
L-83-244; 48-8-1a,b

The ancient flute has four notes. The modern flute, made in two parts, has six holes: to
play it, the smaller tube with its reed of split palm leaf is inserted into the larger one.
These two flutes, separated by different cultures and more than 500 years, exemplify the
continuity of Mesoamerican musical tradition.

PLATE 47

Pottery vessel, rollout view
Maya, Huehuetenango, Guatemala. 7th century A.D. H. 20 cm; Dia. 16.2 cm
12699

In 1960, recognition and analysis of this scene as portraying a blood sacrifice raised questions about then current theories of a completely peaceful Maya and pointed the way to a re-examination of previous interpretations of this civilization. In the upper register, several shamans wearing deity masks and holding pointed instruments squat over strips of bark paper in low bowls. Present-day Maya still pierce themselves to strengthen newly planted seeds of maize. The date given is 9.9.5.0.0 in the Maya Long Count, or A.D. 618. The middle register is a sequence of glyphs common on pottery but not yet deciphered. In the lower register, the profile of a supernatural is shown twice: framed within a glyph, and on its side on the handle of the sacrificial knife. Vessel rollout painting by Mary Louise Baker, Museum artist from 1908 to 1936.

PLATE 48

Pottery figurine
Maya, Jaina Island, Yucatán, Mexico.
A.D. 800. H. 17.2 cm
62-11-1

The Maya elite prized the effect of crossed eyes and artificially flattened heads, as in this figurine of a female in the distinctive style of Jaina pottery. She wears an off-the-shoulder blouse, large bead necklace, bracelets, earflares, and a large central disc on her headband. What may be scarification can be seen on her face.

PLATE 49

Ear flares
Top row: Black tubular pottery, incised band. Copilco, Valley of Mexico. 600–200 B.C. L. 2.9 cm; Dia. 2.2 cm. Obsidian (2). Maya, Chipal, Guatemala. A.D. 1000–1200. Dia. of both. 4.2 cm.
Bottom row: Obsidian. Aztec?, Central Mexico. A.D. 1400–1519. Dia. 2.6 cm.
Jadeite. Teotihuacán, Central Mexico. A.D. 200–600. Dia. 3.4 cm
NA5991; L-83-1055; NA11307a,b; L-144-19

Ear lobes were pierced and the holes gradually enlarged, until even large cylinders could be maneuvered into them. Frequently, additional stone beads would be suspended through the cylinders.

PLATE 50
Red, white, and black painted pottery figurine
Chupícuaro, Central Mexico.
After A.D. 400. H. 24.1 cm
66-30-15

This female figurine has facial paint or tattooing, a high hat, and elaborately patterned clothing.

PLATE 51
Pottery stamps
Left: Flower design. Aztec, Tlatelolco, Valley of Mexico. A.D. 1400–1519. H. 4.2 cm.
Top center: Geometric design. El Tajín, Gulf Coast, Mexico. A.D. 300–900. H. 4.8 cm; W. 9.1 cm. Bottom center: Human face in geometric design. Aztec?, Mexico. A.D. 1400–1519. H. 6.5 cm; W.8 cm.
Right: Monkey design. Aztec, Valley of Mexico. A.D. 1400–1519. H. 6 cm
31-41-59; 34-11-70; 31-41-57; 31-41-58

Pottery stamps were ingeniously designed to transfer their patterns onto cloth and the human body.

PLATE 52

From left: Pottery figurine, elaborate bird headdress, patterned skirt. Guerrero, West Mexico. 100 B.C.–A.D.. 100. H. 14.6 cm. Pottery figurine rattle, with braided or coiled hair. Aztec, Pacific Coast, Mexico. A.D. 1400–1519. H. 12.3 cm. Pottery figurine, painted or tattooed body design. Colima, West Mexico. A.D. 100–300. H. 12.7 cm
64-20-1; 31-41-60; 60-7-15

Although the garments of ancient Mesoamerica have long since disintegrated, the intricately detailed figurines enable us to identify different fashions of clothing, hairstyles, and tattooing.

PLATE 53

Obsidian labrets
Ticoman, Mexico. 1000–300 B.C.
Clockwise, from bottom left:
L. 1.3 cm; L. 2 cm; L. 1.7 cm;
L. 1.4 cm; L. 2.9 cm
NA5995; 58-35-55; 58-35-51; 58-35-52; 58-35-56

Among Mesoamerican elites, it was common to pierce the lower lip for the insertion of decorative shapes made of obsidian, jade, quartz, and other colorful stones. Labrets were inserted from the inside of the lip so that the rounded narrow diameter was seen; the flat extension held the ornament in place on the inside of the lip.

PLATE 54

Pottery ear flares
San Jerónimo? Guerrero, Mexico. Ca. 200–1 B.C. From left: Dia. 2.6 cm; Dia. 1.9 cm
CG-2001-2-12; CG2001-2-13

The decorative surfaces of pottery ear flares were sometimes incised, sometimes
cut in intricate designs, as in these charming examples, probably from coastal
Guerrero.

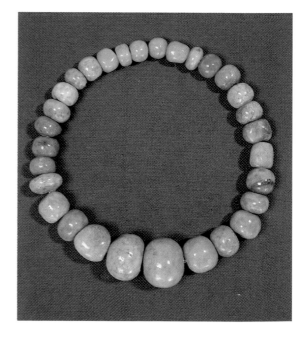

PLATE 55

Jade necklace, 30 beads
Maya, Guatemala.
Ca. A.D. 250–900
NA5997-6026

Jade was precious and supernatural qualities were ascribed to it.
It was associated with water,
maize, and sky. The living wore
jade necklaces and earspools; the
dead had jade beads placed in
their mouths as a sign of rebirth.

PLATE 56

Turquoise, wood, and wax ear ornaments
Jalisco, Mexico. Ca. A.D. 1300–1500.
Top: H. 5.2 cm; W. 6.6 cm. Bottom: H. 5.6 cm; W. 7.7 cm
NA5194

The use of turquoise in mosaic adornments was highly prized by the Aztecs, who valued the workmanship of the West Mexico craftsmen and required turquoise jewelry and masks as tribute items.

PLATE 57

Jade necklace with "Bibhead"
pendant, and 32 beads
Maya, Guatemala. Ca. A.D. 250–900.
Pendant H. 5.7 cm
NA6027, NA6065

Jade was found in only a few
places, was widely traded,
esteemed, and worn by the elite of
all the Mesoamerican cultures.
Some central pendants, like this
"bibhead" design, may have been
heirlooms handed down for
centuries.

PLATE 58

Pottery temple
model: Toltec, Mexico.
A.D. 1000–1200.
H. 11.7 cm
Calcite temple
model: Mezcala,
Guerrero, Mexico.
A.D. 300. H. 11.1 cm
L-83-286; 68-32-1

Miniatures may have
been used as architectural models. The Toltecs, dominant in Central Mexico after the fall of
Teotihuacán, traded widely and absorbed foreign influences. This architectural model reflects
Maya styles with its high pyramid and roofcomb. The people of Guerrero made many small-
scale stone architectonic representations, perhaps as miniature funerary altars.

PLATE 59

Limestone relief carving
Maya, Copán, Honduras. A.D. 750. H. 39.4 cm; W. 52.1 cm
20987

This head of an important celestial deity has jaguar ears, scroll eyebrows, fish fins on his cheeks, and a single filed tooth. This god is often identified with the planet Venus and the sun. Originally, this may have been a shield held by one of the figures on the Hieroglyphic Stairway in Copán, or perhaps a decoration for the building at the top.

PLATE 60

Jadeite plaques
Maya?, Central Mexico. A.D. 400–900.
Left: H. 3.2 cm; W. 5.2 cm. Right: H. 4.3 cm; W. 3.8 cm
12707; 29-150-18

The powerful city of Teotihuacán in Central Mexico flourished from A.D. 100 to about A.D. 700. Its influence can be seen throughout Mesoamerica. These jadeite plaques, found in Central Mexico, have faces carved in a style suggestive of Maya origin, providing evidence for interregional interaction.

65-44-1

PLATE 61

Limestone capstone
Maya, Yucatán or Campeche, Mexico. A.D. 1001. H. 60 cm; W. 32 cm
65-44-1

Maya architecture featured a V-shaped corbeled arch, made without a keystone. Stone was
cut to fit closely, coated with lime plaster, and often painted a bright red. This capstone is
one of a series of horizontally set stones forming the ceiling of a corbel-vaulted chamber.
Painted capstones were usually placed centrally above the doorway.

PLATE 62

Drawing of painting on capstone in Plate 61. On the left is the Maize God, with maize headdress. He is seated on a glyph or cushion with jaguar spots and holds the glyph K'awil, signifying abundance of food. On the right is the Long-nosed God, a common figure in Maya art, usually associated with rain and fertility. The two objects he holds are probably ears of corn. The date recorded, 9 Muluk 11 Uo, is believed to fall in A.D. 1001.

PLATE 63

Pottery effigy vessel
Totonac?, Mixtequilla region, Mexico.
A.D. 250–900. H. 17.5 cm
68-30-1

In one famous episode of the *Popol Vuh,* creation myth of the Guatemalan Highland Maya, a rabbit aids the Hero Twins in an important ball game against the Gods of the Underworld. The spout is broken on this two-part vessel which may at one time have held pulque, a beverage made from the fermented sap of the maguey plant, associated with the rabbit.

PLATE 64

Greenstone yoke, traces of cinnabar pigment
Gulf Coast, Mexico. Ca. A.D. 800. H. 39.3 cm; W. 35.5 cm; Th. 11.5 cm
62-11-3

Horseshoe-shaped belts, called "yokes" by the Spanish conquerors, may have been ceremonial stone replicas of the lighter wicker-and-hide belts actually worn by ball players; other scholars believe that the stone belts were worn during the game. The face carved into the front and ends and the elaborate scroll patterns are typical of the yokes used in central Veracruz.

PLATE 65

Limestone *hachas*
From left: Animal profile head. Maya, western Guatemala. A.D. 250–900. H. 24 cm. Male profile head. Totonac, Tres Zapotes, Gulf Coast, Mexico. A.D. 250–900. H. 18.5 cm. Profile skull. Maya, Santa Rosa, Guatemala. A.D. 250–900. H. 28 cm
12664; 54-36-1; 37-12-5

Hachas, "axe"-shaped thin carved stone heads such as these, may have been worn in the front of the ball player's protective belt as substitutes for trophy heads.

PLATE 66

Volcanic stone *palma*. El Tajín? Gulf Coast, Mexico. Ca. A.D. 800. H. 31.5 cm; W. 20 cm. 62-11-2

Palmas (curved, sculpted ornamental stones) may have been placed upright in the front of the protective belt as the striking surface to start the rubber ball in play. Some scholars argue that wooden *palmas* were worn in the game, and stone only for ceremonial display. Carving on the back of the stone (right) is of a diving figure, a motif that became prevalent in the Yucatán in the centuries immediately preceding the Conquest. The elaborate carving suggests that this stone played an important role in the game and its ceremonies.

PLATE 67

Pottery figurine
Remojadas?, Pánuco, Mexico.
A.D. 200–400. H. 29.8 cm
66-30-19

This figurine illustrates one style of ball game dress. Protective belts, knee guards, and pads were worn. The elaboration of costume undoubtedly reflected the purpose of the game, from the simple clothing shown here to more flamboyant garb required for ceremonial games.

PLATE 68

Two-piece pottery censer
Atzcapotzalco, Central Mexico. A.D. 300–600. H. 49 cm
L-144-9

The rosettes adorning the body of this elaborate incense burner were mold made and mass produced. Similar rosettes in different arrangements have been found on many other censers. The restoration may not be completely accurate, as the censer was found broken into many pieces.

PLATE 69

Tripod vessel
Teotihuacán, Central Mexico. A.D. 300–600. H. 13.5 cm; Dia. 19.4 cm
66-27-16

Tripod vessels are typical of Teotihuacán pottery. The red and black paint is applied after firing; the hollow slab feet have geometric openings. The building illustrated on the body of the vessel uses the traditional Teotihuacán *talud* (slope; slanted wall) and *tablero* (flat, framed table-like panel) architecture.

PLATE 70

Pottery tripod vessel with conical lid topped by an owl. Traces of red paint. Hollow feet, incised geometric design
Teotihuacán, Central Mexico.
A.D. 300–600. H. 21.5 cm; Dia. 12.8 cm
66-27-18a,b

Cylindrical tripod vessels are common in Teotihuacán after A.D. 300. Such vessels are frequently found in other parts of Mesoamerica, evidence for Teotihuacán's widespread influence.

PLATE 71

From the left: Greenstone mask. Toltec?, Central Mexico. A.D. 700–1000. H. 21.5 cm.
Calcite mask. Toltec?, Central Mexico. A.D. 700–1000. H. 17 cm.
Greenstone mask. Teotihuacán, Central Mexico. A.D. 200–700. H. 16 cm
NA10800; NA10799; L-83-154

Teotihuacán burials included stone masks, lifesize or smaller, to cover the face of the dead. Perforations permitted the masks to be attached to the shrouds. The fall of Teotihuacán was followed by the rise of the adjacent Toltec culture, with similar cultural elements, including burial masks. In mask NA10800, the sculptor utilized the natural white spots to represent the eyes.

PLATE 72

Pottery bowl
Aztec, Mexico. A.D. 1350–1519. H. 5.7 cm; Dia. 18.4 cm
L-83-979

The feathered serpent is one of the oldest gods of Mesoamerica, found in very early cultures, as well as among the Aztecs. This bowl's design is "Jewel of the Winds," bold scrolls and a hatched background associated with the god Quetzalcoatl, the feathered serpent.

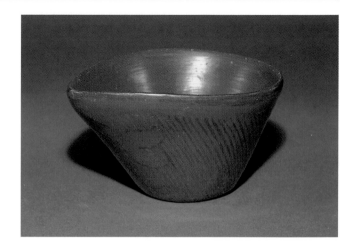

PLATE 73

Pottery cup
Aztec, Mexico.
A.D. 1350–1519.
H. 5.5 cm; L. 10.1 cm
L-83-981

This unusual scuttle-shaped cup is also decorated with the scrolls and hatched background of the "Jewel of the Winds" design. To the Aztecs, Quetzalcoatl was not only a god of winds, but also a patron of rulership and a protector of priests and merchants.

PLATE 74

Polychrome bowl
Cholula, Puebla, Mexico. A.D. 1300–1519. H. 8 cm; Dia. 14.3 cm
68-31-1

The polychrome pottery of Cholula was esteemed highly by all the peoples of Central Mexico, especially the Aztecs.

PLATE 75
Polychrome bowl
Cholula, Puebla, Mexico. A.D. 1300–1519. H. 8 cm; Dia. 14.3 cm
L-82-118

One of the decorations on this bowl is a stylized conch shell, a symbol associated with Quetzalcoatl, the feathered serpent, in his aspect as Ehecatl, the god of wind. Cholula was a pilgrimage center for the worship of this god.

PLATE 76
Redware pipe, incised bird design
Aztec, Mexico. A.D. 1428–1519.
H. 10.8 cm; L. 18 cm
L-144-12

One of the Spanish Conquistadores wrote of the Aztec king that after dinner, servants "placed on the table three painted and decorated pipes filled with liquidambar (a resinous substance, usually derived from the sweetgum tree) and mixed with an herb they call tobacco. After eating...he would take a little smoke from one of these pipes, and with it fall asleep."

PLATE 77

Pottery standing figure
Nayarit, Mexico.
200 B.C.–A.D. 500. H. 39 cm
30-53-1

The standing figure is ornamented with breech-cloth, headband, multi-ple rings in his ears, and a high-relief conch shell at his navel. He holds a cigar-shaped implement in his right hand and a rectangular object in his left hand. Such figures were placed in shaft tombs to replicate the scenes of daily life.

PLATE 78

Stone mask
Mezcala, Guerrero, Mexico.
200 B.C.–A.D. 500. H. 5.2 cm; W. 5.6 cm
66-30-23

The deeply carved angular lines in this
small mask give the face a brooding
aspect.

PLATE 79

Pottery effigy urn
Colima, Mexico. 200 B.C.–A.D. 500. H. 15.2 cm; L. 29 cm
60-7-9

Effigy vessels were placed in shaft tombs and probably held beverages for the dead.
In this figure, the tail is the spout. A small, smooth-haired dog was indigenous to
Central America, and effigies of it figure prominently in ceramics from the Colima
region. They were said to be guides to the Underworld.

PLATE 80
Stone seated figure
Mezcala?, Mexico, 200 B.C.–A.D. 500. H. 12.7 cm; W. 6 cm
63-18-2

The Mezcala culture, centered on the Balsas river, developed a clearly identifiable stoneworking tradition. This small sculpture shows the abstract,
angular quality some Mezcala sculptors gave to their work.

PLATE 81

Pottery effigy urn of a seated figure with animal headdress
Zapotec, Miahuatlán, Oaxaca Valley, Mexico. A.D. 300–700. H. 29 cm
29-41-726

Ceramic funerary urns, characteristic of the cultures of Oaxaca, were made from as early as 600 B.C. and continued to be an important part of tomb furnishings until the Conquest, their function perhaps to provide food or drink to sustain the dead.

PLATE 82

Pottery effigy urn
Zapotec, Oaxaca. Mexico.
A.D. 300–700. H. 20 cm
NA6359

Ceramic details of clothing and headdress were used to identify individual deities, as in this vessel. The figure's central headdress ornament is an early form of the Zapotec Glyph C, identified with Cocijo, the Zapotec rain god.

PLATE 83

Pottery beaker with owl incised in low relief
Zapotec, Oaxaca, Mexico. A.D. 300–700.
H. 18.7 cm
29-41-735

The owl's reputation as a bird of ill omen may stem in part from the fact that it flies at night and frequents caves, believed to be entrances to the Underworld.

PLATE 84

Effigy urn
Zapotec, Cuilapam, Oaxaca, Mexico. A.D. 300–700. H. 30 cm
29-41-705

Instead of attaching the human figure to the urn, here the body of the vessel itself forms the individual.

PLATE 85
Jadeite amulets
Mixtec, Oaxaca, Mexico. A.D. 1000–1521.
From left: H. 2.4 cm. H. 2.6 cm. H. 4.1 cm. H. 3.7 cm
21-41-1102; 21-41-1093; 21-41-1119; 21-41-1109

So widespread was the fame of Mixtec artisans that a group of them lived in a special enclave in Tenochtitlán to serve the Aztec desire for gold, mosaics, and jade. Among the objects they created were diminutive amulets and pendants of jadeite, many with intricate details incised into their minute surfaces.

PLATE 86
Jadeite amulets
Mixtec, Mexico, Oaxaca. A.D. 1000–1521.
From left: H. 7.3 cm. H. 6.6 cm. H. 7.7 cm
NA5969; 29-41-1201; NA5909

PLATE 87

Gadrooned, incised, and painted pottery tripod bowl
Mixtec, Mexico. Ca. A.D. 1300. H. 14.4 cm; Dia. 10.7 cm
61-1-3

The colorful Mixtec pottery style was a popular trade item, which may explain why this vessel was found in Colima, West Mexico, hundreds of miles from the Oaxaca Valley where it was made.

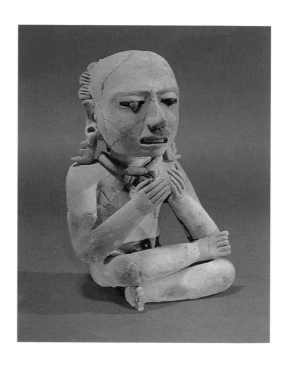

PLATE 88

Pottery seated male figure
Classic Veracruz, Central Veracruz,
Mexico. Ca. A.D. 600. H. 25.5 cm
69-24-2

The figure has elaborate drooping earplugs, a necklace with a four-cornered central jewel, and what may be a shell headband.

PLATE 89

Pottery figurine
Nayarit, Mexico. 200 B.C.–A.D. 500.
H. 20 cm
60-7-10

This seated humpbacked male figure
holds what may be a deer antler,
possibly for use as a crutch. Given
the number of figurines with this
and other kinds of physical abnor-
malities, it would seem that people
with such defects held a special
position in society. What that position was, whether a mark of supernatural power or a more unfavor-
able opinion, is likely to remain
unknown.

PLATE 90

Pottery seated male figure in two
pieces
Classic Veracruz, Veracruz, Mexico.
A.D. 500–700. H. 28 cm
61-8-1a,b

The headdress on this two-piece
seated figure may represent palm
fronds. He wears a cape that was
broken in antiquity. The lower part
of his face is covered with a mask.
The face itself is daubed with black
paint obtained from bitumen, a natural substance that seeps from oil
deposits lying below ground.

PLATE 91

Pottery figure
Remojadas, Veracruz, Mexico.
A.D. 500–700. H. 46 cm
61-1-2

The peoples of the Gulf Coast
developed a wealth of pottery
styles, including large hollow standing figures. This imposing figure
wears elaborate cup-like ear decorations, armlets, anklets, necklace,
and belt. The animal-head headdress,
skin shirt, and the tail of the animal
costume forming a support for the
figure suggest that this may represent a shaman.

PLATE 92

Pottery maskette
Remojadas, Veracruz, Mexico.
A.D. 200–700. H. 9.3 cm
15076

Small maskettes such as this may have
been made as removable parts for
figurines lost in antiquity. The leaf-nose
bat is a frequent motif in Mesoamerican
art and Maya hieroglyphs.

PLATE 93

Pottery maskette
Remojadas, Veracruz, Mexico.
A.D. 200–700. H. 14.5 cm
15079

The elaborate headdress and
dimensional scroll on its forehead suggest a supernatural
character, one as yet unidentified, for this duck-billed
miniature mask.

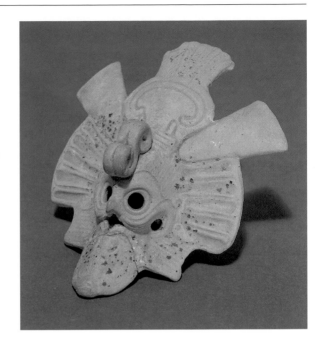

PLATE 94

Pottery mask
Remojadas, Veracruz,
Mexico. A.D. 500–700. H.
15.5 cm
61-1-1

Masks and figurines with "smiling faces" are typical of the Remojadas culture. Unfortunately,
most have not been excavated scientifically, and their function is still uncertain. Many scholars believe that they were designed for ritual purposes, and the facial expression may indi-
cate a hallucinogen-induced trance state.

PLATE 95

Pottery pipe
Aztec, Cholula, Puebla, Mexico.
A.D. 1400–1519.
H. 9 cm; L. 14 cm
NA5592

The pipe represents the figure of
the Old God, called Huehueteotl
by the Aztecs. One of his legs
forms the pipestem and his back
is the bowl. A god of great antiquity, he was a guardian of the
hearth and the household. This is
a variation of the way he is usually shown: seated, tailor fashion,
with a brazier on his head.

PLATE 96

Stone pendants
Maya, Chipal, Guatemala. A.D. 1000–1200. From left: H. 7 cm. H. 5.1 cm. H. 3.6 cm
NA11371; NA11375; NA11373

These stone pendants depict the common theme of "The Long-nosed God," frequently
identified with Chac, the rain god. The motif is also associated with a figure known as the
Jester God, a symbol of rulership.

PLATE 97

Pottery cup
Maya, Chipal, Guatemala. A.D. 1000–1200. H. 18.2 cm; Dia. of cup 12.3 cm
NA11531

Plumbate, the only vitrified pottery in Mesoamerica, was produced on the
Pacific coast of Guatemala and traded widely beginning as early as about A.D.
850. In this example, the figure of the warrior wears the costume and shield
customary in Central Mexico, one of many lines of evidence for interregional
interaction.

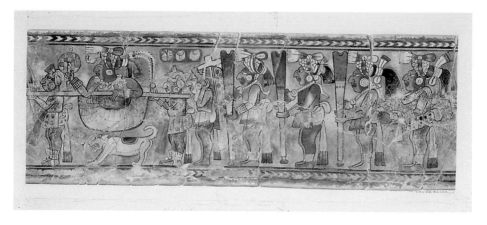

PLATE 98

Polychrome cylinder vase, rollout view
Maya, Ratinlixul, Guatemala. A.D. 650–750? H. 21.2 cm; Dia. 18.5 cm
NA11701

Maya artists created polychrome pottery cylinders of exceptional beauty during the period known as the Late Classic, A.D. 550–850. The Museum has an important collection from the highland site of Chamá, a style immediately identifiable by the chevron design framing the painted narrative scenes. In this famous vessel an elite figure is carried in a litter, followed by retainers carrying a jaguar pelt–covered mat, trumpets or canoe paddles, and what may be a bundle of cloth. Rollout view of vase painted by Mary Louise Baker.

PLATE 99

Pottery effigy whistle
Maya, Chipal, Guatemala.
A.D. 1000–1200. H. 15 cm
NA11571

The warrior holds his captive in his left hand as he raises what appears to be an obsidian knife in his right hand. He is elaborately clothed in a long embroidered loincloth, high hat or headdress, and short cape and is adorned with long earrings, bracelet, and anklets.

PLATE 100

Limestone bowl
Maya, Campeche?, Mexico.
A.D. 300–500. H. 9.5 cm;
Dia. 11.3 cm
64-27-1

Four large godhead glyphs are
carved around the outside of this
bowl from the Yucatán peninsula.

PLATE 101

Pottery polychrome dish, tripod supports
Alta Gracia, Ometepe Island, Greater Nicoya, Nicaragua. A.D. 1350–1520.
H. 12.7 cm; Dia. 22.9 cm
12700

The people of Nicaragua created a distinctive style of pottery, as seen in this
dramatic painted tripod vessel. On the inside of the dish a long-lipped supernatural stands with arms extended, surrounded on the side of the dish by
birds with wings outstretched.

PLATE 102

Pottery cylinder vase, rollout view. Maya, Chamá, Guatemala. A.D. 700–900. H. 23.5 cm; Dia. 15 cm
38-14-1

Known as the "Chamá Vase," this vessel is in excellent condition except for a single crack. This is one of the series of rollout paintings by Mary Louise Baker. Each of the figures in the scene on this vase is shown with glyphs nearby, suggesting that they are identified by name. The two principal figures are painted black, the color associated with Ek Chuah, the Maya god of merchants. They face each other over a kneeling figure whose right hand is at his left shoulder in a gesture believed to symbolize submission. The standing figure wearing the jaguar-skin cape may be a chief or shaman. The figure to his right is identified by glyphs as "young sprout" or heir.

PLATE 103

Jadeite and greenstone necklace with
effigy pendant
Chorotegan, Costa Rica. A.D. 900–1520.
H. of central pendant 10.3 cm
39-24-26 to 39-24-51

The bluegreen jade of Costa Rica was
especially valued by the Olmec and con-
tinued to be prized by later cultures. The arrangement of these beads and the central effigy
pendant is a modern conception of how these ancient pieces might have been worn.

PLATE 104

Marble dish
Ulúa Valley, Honduras. A.D. 600–1000. H. 4.5 cm; Dia. 13 cm
NA5529

This dish is carved with the mat design, symbol of rulership among the Maya, and a leaf-nose
bat, a motif used frequently in art and glyphs. Unfortunately, while some Ulúa Valley marble
vessels have been found in tombs and excavated scientifically, most have not, thus severely
limiting the knowledge they might provide.

PLATE 105

Marble cylinder vase
Ulúa Valley, Honduras. A.D. 600–1000.
H. 17.3 cm; Dia. 13.6 cm
NA5527

The people of the Ulúa Valley in north-western Honduras developed an art style that drew on traditions of the Maya as well as the lesser-known cultures of Central America, such as the Lenca and Paya. The finely carved marble vases with elaborate glyphlike scroll designs and animal-shaped handles are among the best-known artifacts from this region.

PLATE 106

Marble tripod bowl
Ulúa Valley, Honduras. A.D. 600–1000. H. 11.8 cm; Dia. 15 cm
NA5528

The handles and the tripod supports for this bowl are animal heads similar to those of the jaguars that form the handles of the marble cylinders. Close scrutiny of the relief decoration on this bowl and the cylinders reveals faces hidden amid the scrolls.

PLATE 107

Marble cylinder vase
Ulúa Valley, Honduras. A.D. 600–1000. H. 25 cm; Dia. 15.9 cm
NA5526

These vessels were traded into the Maya region and have been found at sites in Belize and the Guatemala lowlands. Their use appears to have been limited to elite ceremonies.

PLATE 108A

Spondylus oyster shell amulet
Ulúa Valley, Honduras. A.D. 600–1000. L. 11.4 cm
NA 5572

Honduran craftsmen excelled in working the plentiful marine shells, as this beautiful carving of a caiman attests. Representations of reptilians (crocodiles, snakes, turtles) with a second head instead of a tail are found throughout Mesoamerica. Among the Maya, the ruler is frequently shown holding a two-headed serpent bar.

PLATE 108B

A closeup reveals the artist's skill in incorporating the shell's discoloration to portray a ravaged human face at the caiman's tail.